D1376903

a pictorial biography

IKE

a pictorial biography

TEXT BY WILLIAM F. LONGGOOD

PICTURE EDITOR: SIMONE DARO GOSSNER

TIME-LIFE BOOKS, NEW YORK

IKE, A PICTORIAL BIOGRAPHY

Editor: Charles Osborne
Designer: Edward Frank
Chief Researcher: Jane Alexander
Researchers: Evelyn H. Constable, Maria Livanos,
Patricia T. Smalley, Sigrid von Huene
Picture Researcher: Joan T. Lynch
Copyreader: David L. Harrison

The editors of this book are indebted to John S. D. Eisenhower and Professor James P. Shenton of Columbia University. The following individuals and departments of Time Inc. gave valuable assistance in the preparation of the book: Editorial Production, Robert W. Boyd Jr.; Editorial Reference, Peter Draz; Picture Collection, Doris O'Neil; Photographic Laboratory, George Karas; TIME-LIFE News Service, Richard M. Clurman.

Published simultaneously in Canada.
Library of Congress catalogue card number 68-54473.

CONTENTS

A LEGACY OF THE FRONTIER

1

Dwight was just 20 when this picture was taken in 1910, the year before he left home for West Point. Flanking him are two of his younger brothers, Earl, 12, and Milton, 10. In front of their parents, David and Ida Stover Eisenhower, stands Ike's dog Flip, his constant boyhood companion. Flip deserted a passing circus, foregoing its glamour for a more secure life with the Eisenhowers.

Dwight David Eisenhower was one of the most powerful and important men of the 20th Century. During the last quarter-century of his life, he was Supreme Commander of the great Allied armies that helped crush Nazi Germany, president of a great university, commander of the western military alliance against Communism and for two terms President of the United States. Yet it may be that he will be best remembered not for what he did during his long career, but for what he was. For millions throughout the world he was the embodiment of human decency—an honest, sincere, warm man without the slightest trace of pomposity. As a soldier he led vast military forces without a hint of militaristic strut. As President he was remarkable for his candor, and for his cheerful faith that the nation and its people were fundamentally sound. Vast numbers of his countrymen, and of people in other nations, responded to his optimism and openness with trust, respect and love. He was revered not for the positions he held, but for himself.

Eisenhower's extraordinary career was a classic American success story. He was a poor country boy—if his birthplace was not exactly a log cabin, it was a simple frame house in a small town—and he rose to the pinnacle of world power through his own industry and intelligence. Yet this storybook quality could hardly have been detected in his early years. He was an indifferent student, often in scrapes. At the U.S. Military Academy his grades were unexceptional (and his discipline rating was among the lowest in his class); his first assignments as a young officer employed him mainly as a football coach. But his strength of character, his perseverance and, most of all, his quick mind did not go unnoticed in the intimate, family-like atmosphere of the post-World War I Army. He was assigned to ever-more-demanding positions, building the reputation that, when the crisis of World War II required an exceptional leader, made him an obvious choice.

Such opportunity came to a personality shaped for it by the ideals of the frontier, which, though physically dead when young Dwight was growing up in turn-of-the-century Kansas, was spiritually still very much

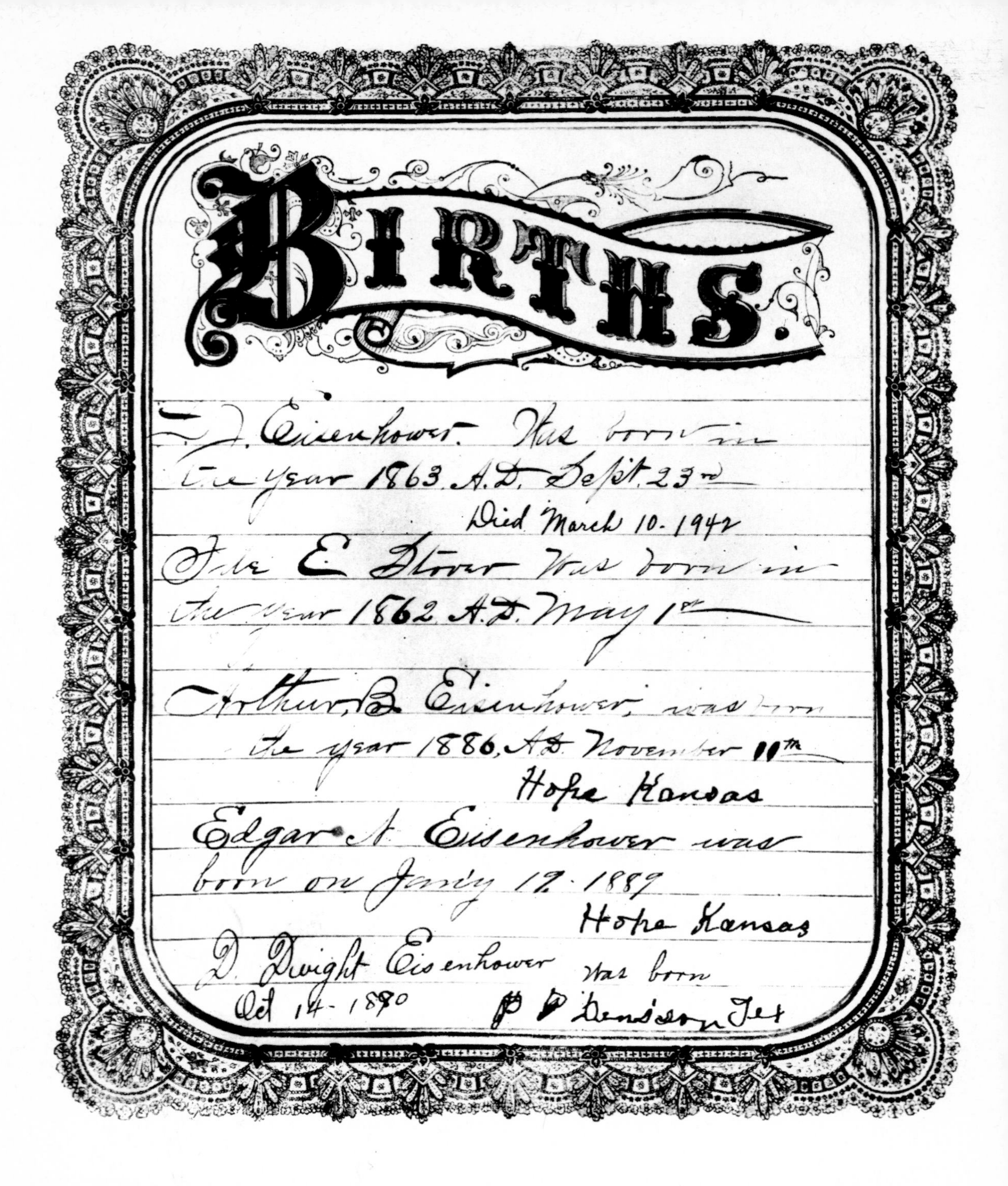
BIRTHS.

D. J. Eisenhower. Was born in the year 1863. A.D. Sept. 23rd
Died March 10. 1942
Ida E. Stover was born in the year 1862. A.D. May 1st
Arthur B. Eisenhower, was born the year 1886. A.D. November 11th
Hope Kansas
Edgar N. Eisenhower was born on Jany 19. 1889
Hope Kansas
D. Dwight Eisenhower was born
Oct 14 - 1890 P O Denison Tex

alive. Eisenhower was raised to cherish what are now called the old-fashioned virtues of honesty, ambition and work. It was Ida, his mother, whom Eisenhower later credited with giving him the values that guided his career. Of her he once said, "My father failed twice. Each time my mother smiled and worked harder."

Dwight Eisenhower was descended from Pennsylvania pioneers of Swiss-German ancestry who had moved west to Kansas, but he was born in 1890 in the little prairie town of Denison, Texas, wnere his father had gone after the failure of his general store in Hope, Kansas. A year later the family, homesick for Kansas, returned to settle in Abilene, not long since a famous cowtown.

The Eisenhower boys, supplementing the family income by peddling vegetables to the middle-class housewives of Abilene, were often snubbed. Of their pioneer background, the Eisenhowers were proud. As for their lack of status and affluence, they thought of it as no more than one among many obstacles—to be conquered in terms of the frontier values they all took for granted. Chief among the tenets sacred to those values was, of course, the unquestioned availability of opportunity. For Dwight Eisenhower, given his background, character and upbringing, opportunity seemed to lead almost inevitably through West Point to unprecedented military responsibilities—and finally to the very highest office.

Statistics of their life were recorded in the Eisenhowers' Bible. Listed are David and Ida and their first three sons. Originally Ike was named David Dwight, but his mother called him Dwight to avoid confusion with his father. Later Ike called himself Dwight David.

For his first picture, taken in Abilene when he was three, Dwight (lower right), who had not graduated to boy's clothes, wore a dress and a solemn expression. Behind him are his brothers, Edgar, four, and Arthur, seven, who held Roy, then the baby of the family.

In 1891 the Eisenhowers bought a modest frame house on the wrong side of the tracks. The house (behind the car) stood in the "poor" South Side of Abilene next to the Union Pacific and Sante Fe right of way. But to the family, which had been living in a tiny rented place nearby, the house, which had a yard, seemed a castle. Ida Eisenhower said to a neighbor, "I've been married almost 14 years and I am 36 years old. For the first time we have a home where my children will have room to play. I am most thankful."

On their three-acre plot the Eisenhowers raised vegetables that "Little Ike" and his brother Edgar (called "Big Ike" by schoolmates) sold to well-to-do North Side families across the tracks. At right Dwight appears (second from left) in the fourth grade class picture of the Lincoln School. Unlike his classmates, he wore overalls; once, to his humiliation, he had to wear his mother's high-button shoes to school; his own had worn out and there was no money in the budget for new ones.

GROWING UP POOR IN ABILENE

In 1902, when Ike was 12, the Eisenhowers dressed up in their Sunday best for the formal family portrait at right. Standing next to Dwight (far left) were Edgar, Earl, Arthur and Roy. Between their parents was Milton, then three; he had been kept in long curls because David and Ida had so desperately wanted a girl. The closely knit family placed such sentimental store by the photo that when they held a reunion 24 years later they all posed in the same positions (above). Even after Ike became famous, Ida Eisenhower would never admit to any difference in the achievements of her boys. Asked when Ike was Supreme Commander if she was not proud of her son, she replied, "Which one?"

BEGINNINGS OF A LOVE FOR SPORTS

All the Eisenhower boys had household chores to perform, and in addition they found odd jobs to help the family finances and make some pocket money. Along with school, these labors left little time for play. But occasionally, as proven by the rare photograph at left, Ike (foreground) and his friends went on camping trips to nearby Smoky Hill River, better known to them as "Mud Creek."

Above all recreations, Dwight loved team sports; he was known as a fierce competitor, on the field and off. Once he was goaded by some older boys into fighting the North Side champion; they pounded one another for more than an hour until his opponent gasped, "Ike, I can't lick you."

Dwight showed the same spirit when he played baseball and football for Abilene High School; in the picture of the 1909 baseball team he appears in the center of the first row. He loved baseball so ardently that he once almost risked his life to be able to play. A scratched knee turned into blood poisoning, and the doctor wanted to amputate his leg. "I'd rather be dead than crippled and not able to play ball," he cried. Before lapsing into delirium, he made Edgar promise that under no circumstances would he let them amputate his leg. For two days and nights Edgar stood guard until Ike had conquered the infection—without the dreaded operation.

In his senior year, Dwight wrote an article, reproduced below, for the high school annual, telling how he and others started an athletic association. In a brisk, unselfconscious third person he duly reported his own election as president of the association and his position as right end on the football team. On other pages, the yearbook predicted that Dwight would become a history professor at Yale, while Edgar would twice be elected President of the United States.

Athletics

By Dwight Eisenhower

EARLY in the fall of 1908, the High School boys organized an Athletic Association for the year. After electing Dwight Eisenhower president, Harry Makins vice-president and Herbert Sommers secretary and treasurer, we proceeded to do business.

Deciding not to play any base ball in the fall, we started on football at once. Bruce Hurd was elected captain, and soon a large number of candidates for the squad were out working. After two weeks of hard work, Captain Hurd decided on the following team:

Left end	Huffman
Left tackle	Ingersoll
Left guard	Pattin
Center	Funk
Right guard	Weckle
Right tackle	Hurd
Right end	D. Eisenhower
Quarter	Merrifield
Left half	Makins
Right half	Sommers
Full back	E. Eisenhower

We were deprived of our coach, but nevertheless, turned out a very creditable team. Unfortunately, however, only four games were played during the season, not giving the team a chance to prove its ability. But for the games that were played, the students supported the team loyally, and time and again the boys surmounted great difficulties, cheered on by the fierce enthusiasm displayed by our rooters.

After the football season closed, we had to spend the winter dreaming of past victories and future glories, for A. H. S. boasts of no indoor gymnasium, and basket ball was never played here. But we improved the condition of the Association itself, by drawing up a constitution, which makes the organization a permanent one, and each year it will be simply a question of electing new officers.

Thanking the citizens of the town who have taken such an interest in the High School Athletics, and also our fellow classmates for their loyalty to us, we are yours for future victories on the gridiron by teams of dear old A. H. S.

FOOTBALL SCHEDULE

Abilene vs. Junction City at Junction City.
Abilene vs. Junction City at Abilene.
Abilene vs. Chapman at Abilene.
Abilene vs. Agricultural College at Abilene.

—THE VAULTER—

WEST POINT—

Major General Thomas H. Barry

Abilene, Kansas,
Aug. 20, 1910.

Sen. Bristow,
Salina, Kans.

Dear Sir:

I would very much like to enter either the school at Annapolis, or the one at West Point. In order to do this, I must have an appointment to one of these places and so I am writing to you in order to secure the same.

I have graduated from high school and will be nineteen years of age this fall.

If you find it posible to appoint me to one of these schools, your kindness will certainly be appreciated by me.

Trusting to hear from you, concerning this matter, at your earliest conveniance, I am,

Respectfully yours,
Dwight Eisenhower.

Captain John M. Bowyer

OR ANNAPOLIS?

Upon graduation from high school in 1909, Dwight hoped to go to college—eventually. Then a friend of his, Everett (Swede) Hazlett, encouraged Ike to join him in seeking an appointment to Annapolis. As Dwight considered the possibility of getting a free college education, it made sense. Like a gambler hedging his bet, Ike wrote a letter (left) to Senator Joseph L. Bristow (right), a Kansas Republican, requesting an appointment to "either the school at Annapolis, or the one at West Point."

Senator Bristow held competitive examinations for applicants (an unusual practice at the time), and Ike scored first for Annapolis, second for West Point. At the moment, Dwight's future was in delicate balance between West Point, then headed by Major General Thomas H. Barry (upper left), and Annapolis, under command of Captain John M. Bowyer (above). But to Ike's disappointment, it turned out that he would soon be 21—too old to enter Annapolis with his friend Swede Hazlett. Then came fateful news: the boy who had beaten him in the West Point exams had failed the physical tests. Dwight thus became first choice. Subsequently he passed the Academy's stiff entrance exam and was ordered to report for duty.

His pacifist mother was disappointed that one of her sons had picked a military career, but she left the decision to Ike and his own conscience. "It is your choice," she said. In the summer of 1911 he bade her farewell and departed for the Military Academy. "She saw me off, and then went to her room. Milton told me later that for the first time in his life he heard Mother cry."

CULTIVATING A CAREER

2

To young Dwight Eisenhower, the opportunity to attend the Military Academy was not so much the door to a career of public service as a way to acquire a college degree. Indeed, in his years at the Point, Ike showed little promise of his future military greatness. Primarily interested in athletics, he played baseball and football, winning recognition as one of the most promising backs in the East until a knee injury benched him permanently. "I have often wondered why, at that moment, I did not give increased attention to studies," Eisenhower later wrote. "As the academic record attests, I gave less. . . . Life seemed to have little meaning." But a chance to coach the junior varsity football squad helped Ike pull himself together; and his performance in that job, combined with the drive he had shown before his injury, outweighed his scholastic record. His potential did not go unnoticed. One report on Eisenhower at the Point asserted that he was "born to command."

Upon leaving the Academy, Ike's first assignment was to the 19th Infantry Regiment stationed at Fort Sam Houston, near San Antonio, Texas. There he displayed for a time the same devil-may-care attitude that had characterized him at West Point—at least until he met and married Mamie Doud, a pretty visitor from Denver. The serious pursuit of his career dates more or less from his wedding day. When World War I erupted he desperately tried to join a combat unit overseas, but to his chagrin he was kept at home to train troops. He was so good at the job, however, that he was given command of the Tank Corps Training Center at Camp Colt, Pennsylvania, which had 600 officers, 9,000 troops and, eventually, three small French-made tanks.

Only three years out of the Point, Ike was a temporary lieutenant colonel. But the sense of success ended with the fighting. Tragedy entered his life—the death of his young son, born during the War. One routine assignment followed another; at one point, he became so discouraged that he considered quitting.

He need not have worried. In the exclusive club that was the peacetime Army, Eisenhower was already being watched and groomed. In 1925, Ike attended the Command and General Staff School at Leavenworth, emerging first in a class of 275 that included some of the Army's most promising young officers. From that time, he was on his way.

As one of West Point's outstanding young football prospects, Ike's picture was taken in the traditional high kicking pose during the 1912 season. Among his assets as an Army halfback (he weighed about 174 pounds) were speed and aggressiveness.

THE POINT: GOODBYE TO BOYHOOD

However intent on books Ike appeared in the picture below, he was chided for his unscholarly devotion to eating and sleeping in the cadet yearbook, "The Howitzer" (right). In the academy record, Ike wound up 61st in academic standing among his 164 classmates; in conduct he was 125th, with a whopping total of 211 demerits. By contrast, his classmate, the future General Omar Bradley, was 44th in scholarship and sixth in conduct.

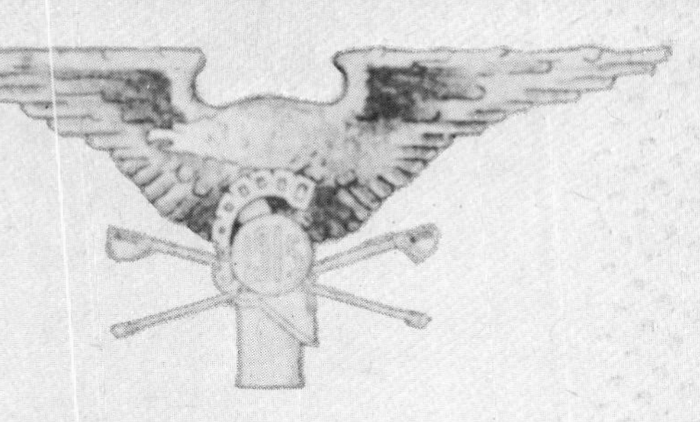

DWIGHT DAVID EISENHOWER

ABILENE, KANSAS

Senatorial Appointee, Kansas
"Ike"

Corporal, Sergeant, Color Sergeant; A.B., B.A., Sharpshooter; Football Squad (3, 2), "A" in Football; Baseball Squad (4); Cheer Leader; Indoor Meet (4, 3).

"Now, fellers, it's just like this. I've been asked to say a few words this evening about this business. Now, me and Walter Camp, we think—"
—Himself

THIS is Señor Dwight David Eisenhower, gentlemen, the terrible Swedish-Jew, as big as life and twice as natural. He claims to have the best authority for the statement that he is the handsomest man in the Corps and is ready to back up his claim at any time. At any rate you'll have to give it to him that he's well-developed abdominally—and more graceful in pushing it around than Charles Calvert Benedict. In common with most fat men, he is an enthusiastic and sonorous devotee of the King of Indoor Sports, and roars homage at the shrine of Morpheus on every possible occasion.

However, the memory of man runneth back to the time when the little Dwight was but a slender lad of some 'steen years, full of joy and energy and craving for life and movement and change. 'Twas then that the romantic appeal of West Point's glamour grabbed him by the scruff of the neck and dragged him to his doom. Three weeks of Beast gave him his fill of life and movement and as all the change was locked up at the Cadet Store out of reach, poor Dwight merely consents to exist until graduation shall set him free.

At one time he threatened to get interested in life and won his "A" by being the most promising back in Eastern football—but the Tufts game broke his knee and the promise. Now Ike must content himself with tea, tiddledywinks and talk, at all of which he excels. Said prodigy will now lead us in a long, loud yell for—Dare Devil Dwight, the Dauntless Don.

Pausing during the traditional visit of the West Point graduating class to the Gettysburg battlefield, Ike and his classmates sit for an informal picture on the steps of the Lutheran Church (famous class members are identified by numbers keyed at right).

1
EISENHOWER

2
BRADLEY

3
VAN FLEET

THE CLASS THE STARS FELL ON

OMAR NELSON BRADLEY
General of the Army

In Ike's West Point class of 1915, celebrated as "The Class the stars fell on," were 59 cadets (of a total of 164) who became generals (16 more than the class of 1917, its nearest competitor). The pictures on this page show the highest ranking officers as they looked in the 1915 edition of *The Howitzer,* the Academy yearbook. The chart at the right lists the men who became generals, their rank and class standing. In most cases a cadet's standing was not a barometer of how well he would do later on. Ike, for example, was 61st and Bradley 44th; John Keliher stood 159th but became a brigadier general. At the far right are the three cadets who stood first, last and in the middle of the class of 1915—and their biographies.

DWIGHT DAVID EISENHOWER
General of the Army

JAMES ALWARD VAN FLEET
General

JOSEPH TAGGART McNARNEY
General

STAFFORD LEROY IRWIN
Lieutenant General

THOMAS BERNARD LARKIN
Lieutenant General

JOSEPH MAY SWING
Lieutenant General

HENRY SPIESE AURAND
Lieutenant General

GEORGE EDWARD STRATEMEYER
Lieutenant General

JOHN WILLIAM LEONARD
Lieutenant General

HUBERT REILLY HARMON
Lieutenant General

1	W.E.R. COVELL		★★			
5	J. S. BRAGDON		★★			
6	G. J. RICHARDS		★★			
9	L. W. MILLER	★				
10	D. L. WEART		★★			
13	J. F. CONKLIN	★				
16	W. F. TOMPKINS		★★			
19	D. A. DAVISON		★★			
20	H. S. AURAND			★★★		
21	T. B. LARKIN			★★★		
23	J. A. LESTER		★★			
24	M. J. YOUNG	★				
26	H. BEUKEMA	★				
29	E. A. ZUNDEL	★				
30	C. W. HOWARD	★				
31	C. M. BUSBEE	★				
32	A. W. WALDRON		★★			
37	H. B. SAYLER		★★			
38	J. M. SWING			★★★		
39	C. W. RYDER		★★			
40	S. L. IRWIN			★★★		
41	J. T. McNARNEY				★★★★	
42	P. MENOHER	★				
44	O. N. BRADLEY					★★★★★
45	P. J. MUELLER		★★			
46	L. S. HOBBS		★★			
48	E. B. LYON		★★			
53	C. C. BANK	★				
55	V. EVANS		★★			
56	R. B. WOODRUFF		★★			
61	D. D. EISENHOWER					★★★★★
63	H. PEABODY	★				
68	E. L. NAIDEN	★				
73	R. W. STRONG	★				
75	J. B. WOGAN		★★			
77	C. H. TENNEY	★				
82	E. C. WALLINGTON	★				
84	J. W. LEONARD			★★★		
92	J. A. VAN FLEET				★★★★	
95	W. W. HESS, JR.	★				
96	M. F. DAVIS	★				
103	H. R. HARMON			★★★		
104	B. G. FERRIS	★				
106	T. G. HEARN		★★			
109	R. M. HOWELL	★				
110	H. J. F. MILLER		★★			
120	J. N. ROBINSON	★				
122	V. V. TAYLOR	★				
124	T. J. HANLEY, JR.		★★			
128	L. A. WALTON		★★			
129	R. P. COUSINS		★★			
134	V. E. PRICHARD		★★			
137	A. H. GILKESON	★				
145	N. RANDOLPH	★				
147	G. E. STRATEMEYER			★★★		
150	F. W. BOYE	★				
151	L. H. WATSON		★★			
158	A. A. WHITE		★★			
159	J. KELIHER	★				

William Edward Raab Covell, of Washington, D.C., was first in the class of 1915. "The Howitzer" respectfully observed that "if he doesn't come across with a subway to Europe or a railway to the moon we shall be disappointed." Covell served in the Corps of Engineers with distinction, retiring from the Army in 1948 as a two-star general.

Edward Caswell Wallington, who hailed from Vineland, New Jersey, stood 82nd among his classmates—the midpoint in standings. "The Howitzer" remarked that he was fond of women and was a good fellow, "always ready to walk a guard tour for the man who is dragging [dating]. . . ." Wallington retired in 1951 as a brigadier general.

Charles Curtiss Herrick, of Sayre, Oklahoma, wound up last in his class. "The Howitzer" said of Herrick: "Nature intended him for a drum major. Fate decided he should be a cadet and God knows how he has remained one. . . ." He served with the infantry until 1922, retiring as a major. But he returned to active duty in World War II, and retired in 1951 as a colonel.

When the newly commissioned Second Lieutenant Eisenhower reported to Fort Sam Houston, he was known as a poker-playing woman hater. Within a month, he met 18-year-old Mamie Doud, a demure and pretty visitor who daintily balanced her parasol for this 1915 snapshot. Falling in love, Ike gave Mamie his class ring on Valentine's Day, 1916; in July they were married at her home in Denver. Ike was strikingly handsome as he posed with his radiant new bride (left) upon their return to San Antonio. The newlyweds' first home was his tiny bachelor quarters, where they entertained so much that the 3-room apartment became known among the fort's young officers as the "Club Eisenhower."

STARTING A MARRIAGE AT FORT SAM HOUSTON

FRUSTRATIONS OF A GOOD SOLDIER

From the ports of the United States, thousands of young Americans, like those shown above boarding a troopship, went off to war. In

Eisenhower's pleas for overseas duty in 1918 were ignored by the Army. The picture below reveals the disappointment and frustration of a difficult period that continued after the War.

November 1918, Ike was finally scheduled to join them—but the armistice intervened and Eisenhower, balked of his dream, stayed home.

"During the first World War every one of my frantic efforts to get to the scene of action had been defeated. . . ."

THE SLOW PROCESS OF GROWTH BETWEEN WARS

The return of peace came as a letdown for a man whose life for more than two years had been preparation for war. Suddenly Ike found himself shorn of his command, reduced from his wartime rank of lieutenant colonel to his permanent grade of captain. Mamie was in Denver with their baby, Doud Dwight (nicknamed Icky), who had been born during the War, and Ike was lonely. The Army was being cut to the bone by economies. The future looked bleak.

But if Captain Eisenhower needed proof that his career was not stagnating it soon came.

At his post at Camp Meade, in Maryland, Ike became friendly with a group of senior tank officers who had seen action in France. The one Ike became closest to was a young cavalry colonel named George S. Patton Jr., whose soldierly bearing contrasted oddly with a high squeaking voice.

Eisenhower and Patton had a common enthusiasm for tanks, and together they developed revolutionary theories about their use. In World War I, tanks had been mobile machine gun platforms used primarily to support infantry. But Ike and Patton thought that tanks should be a fast, independent arm, "that they should attack by surprise and in mass. . . ." In their enthusiasm for this unorthodox use of tanks, both young officers began writing articles for military journals—an enterprise that met a cold reception from their superiors. Ike was called before the Chief of Infantry and told firmly that his ideas were not only wrong but dangerous and that he would do well to keep them to himself; if he did not he would be court-martialed. Patton was told virtually the same thing by his boss.

As a result of their dressing-down, Ike and Patton were forced to communicate with each other almost like conspirators. They became closer than ever, and the relationship was to have immediate consequences for Eisenhower. Through Patton, he met Brigadier General Fox Conner *(right)*, considered one of the best brains in the Army; Conner had been operations officer for General Pershing in France, where Patton had met him. At a dinner party in the Pattons' home, the general questioned Ike about his radical ideas on tanks and expressed interest in them. Ike thought no more of it until a few months later, when Conner, newly assigned to the Army in the Panama Canal Zone, asked if he would like to go as his executive officer. Ike was enthusiastic, but the War Department turned down his request for a transfer.

Meanwhile, Dwight had been spending much of his time at Meade coaching football; while he found this a frustrating assignment, he and Mamie and Icky were enjoying life as a family. For their young son the army camp was a thrilling place. He was devoted to the soldiers, and they bought him a complete tank uniform and took him along on drills. Ike confessed that he was inclined to show Icky off at the slightest excuse, "or without one, for that matter. . . . I'm sure I strutted a bit and Mamie was thoroughly happy. . . ."

Then, suddenly, there was tragedy. The Eisenhowers hired a maid who, unknown to them, had recently recovered from scarlet fever. Icky caught the disease from her. Ike gave a heartbreaking account of what happened to Icky: "During his illness, the doctor did not allow me into his room. But there was a porch on which I was allowed to sit and I could look into his room and wave to him. Occasionally, they would let me come to the door just to speak to Icky. . . . At the turn of the year, we lost our firstborn son. . . ."

Both Mamie and Ike were crushed. More than half a century later he remembered Icky's death as "the greatest disappointment and disaster in my life, the one I have never been able to forget completely. . . . My wife and I have arranged that when it comes our time to be buried, to be laid away in our final resting place, we shall have him with us."

If their grief could not be assuaged, at least they

soon found some relief in an unexpected change of scenery. General Fox Conner, who had earlier requested Eisenhower as his executive officer and been turned down, asked once more. Conner, a friend of General Pershing (then Army Chief of Staff), used his influence to cut through red tape and finally succeeded in getting Eisenhower assigned to his staff. Ike reported to Panama in January 1922.

It was General Conner who got Ike really interested in military history, giving him a perspective and knowledge of campaigns waged by great leaders. He trained Ike to read and then think about military history. Conner would question him about strategic and tactical decisions, asking why and under what conditions they were made, and what might have happened had different decisions been made.

For nearly three years the general and his young subordinate talked not only about war but about people and life. For Ike it was "a sort of graduate school in military affairs and the humanities," and many times later he acknowledged his "incalculable debt" to Conner.

If Eisenhower needed anything to increase his happiness during this period, he found it in the birth, on August 3, 1923, of his second son, John. The following year Ike returned to the States, bearing with him two admonitions from Conner: that there was sure to be another world war, and he should prepare himself for it. Second, that he should try to wangle an assignment under a certain Colonel George C. Marshall. Conner predicted that the next war would be fought beside allies, and asserted that Marshall knew more about arranging allied commands than any man he knew; he described Marshall as "nothing short of a genius."

Ike, then a major, was reassigned to Camp Meade and picked up where he had left off before departing to Panama three years earlier—coaching football. Soon, with Fox Conner operating behind the scenes, Ike was given one of the Army's choicest plums; he was ordered to report to the Command and General Staff School at Fort Leavenworth.

The Panama experience with Fox Conner paid off handsomely. Ike, after a year at the school, was graduated at the top of his class. Now he had a new status—as a young man on his way up. In this time of preparation and growing, Fox Conner remained Eisenhower's guide and patron; he had Eisenhower assigned to the Battle Monuments Commission, a prestigious job because the Commission was headed by General Pershing. Ike's job was to write a guidebook to the World War I battlefields in Europe. During the assignment he was stationed in Washington, where he got to know many important government officials. Upon finishing the guidebook, he received a glowing letter of commendation from Pershing. Ike was so proud of this tribute, reproduced above, that he sent it to his parents with the inscription, "To my mother and father Mr. and Mrs. D. J. Eisenhower, with the love and devotion of their son Dwight."

A short time later, in 1927, he was assigned to another school that was the goal of virtually every Army officer: the War College in Washington. In 1928 Ike was sent to Europe to write a revised edition of the guidebook. He visited the battlefields, traveling leisurely over the path of past violence, now lush farmlands and tranquil forests, getting to know the country and its people; frequently he would stop off and eat with workmen he met, sharing his lunch and a bottle of wine with them. In that bright summer before the year of the Crash, France was prosperous and—like the rest of Europe—bent on peace. Never had the admonition of Fox Conner to prepare for a new holocaust seemed less urgent.

THE AMERICAN BATTLE MONUMENTS COMMISSION

State, War, and Navy Building
Washington
August 15, 1927.

Major General Robert H. Allen,
Chief of Infantry,
Washington, D.C.

My dear General Allen:

The detail of Major Dwight D. Eisenhower, who has been assisting the American Battle Monuments Commission in preparing the guide book, expires today. I wish to take this occasion to express my appreciation of the splendid service, which he has rendered since being with us.

In the discharge of his duties, which were most difficult, and which were rendered even more difficult by reason of the short time available for their completion, he has shown superior ability not only in visualizing his work as a whole but in executing its many details in an efficient and timely manner. What he has done was accomplished only by the exercise of unusual intelligence and constant devotion to duty.

With kindest regards, I am

Sincerely yours,
(Signed) John J. Pershing
Chairman.

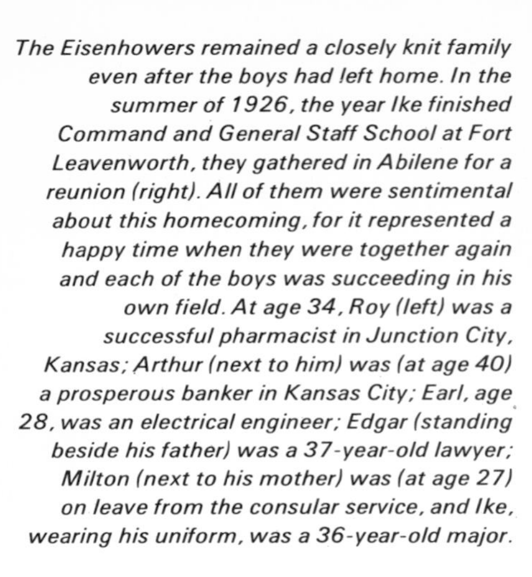

The Eisenhowers remained a closely knit family even after the boys had left home. In the summer of 1926, the year Ike finished Command and General Staff School at Fort Leavenworth, they gathered in Abilene for a reunion (right). All of them were sentimental about this homecoming, for it represented a happy time when they were together again and each of the boys was succeeding in his own field. At age 34, Roy (left) was a successful pharmacist in Junction City, Kansas; Arthur (next to him) was (at age 40) a prosperous banker in Kansas City; Earl, age 28, was an electrical engineer; Edgar (standing beside his father) was a 37-year-old lawyer; Milton (next to his mother) was (at age 27) on leave from the consular service, and Ike, wearing his uniform, was a 36-year-old major.

John Eisenhower was about 18 months old when this picture was taken of him with his mother. Ike said he was almost the image of their son who had died.

201

A COURSE IN LEADERSHIP

3

The armies of the twentieth century are run by staff officers. In the heat of wartime, the flamboyance or skill of a field commander—a Rommel, a Patton, a Montgomery—may raise him temporarily above his fellows. But over the long haul, the reputations that count are made not in the foxholes but at headquarters.

To this axiom, Eisenhower was no exception. Indeed, his first assignment upon returning from his battlefield tour of Europe in 1929 was an administrative post in the office of the Assistant Secretary of War. In this role he was in close contact with General Douglas MacArthur, then Army Chief of Staff. For the next nine years MacArthur was to be the most dominant force in Ike's life. Almost from the start, Eisenhower found himself embroiled in the controversy that always marked MacArthur's career. Ike's initiation came when unemployed veterans of World War I marched on Washington to demand payment of a promised bonus. MacArthur drove the bonus marchers out of the capital, exceeding his orders and bringing down a storm of criticism.

In 1933, MacArthur made Ike his personal military assistant, a job that Eisenhower often found trying but also rewarding. In 1935 MacArthur was appointed military adviser to the Philippine government, then preparing for independence, and insisted on taking Ike with him. As MacArthur's executive officer in the Philippines, he worked closely with the country's top leaders, particularly President Manuel Quezon; he also traveled extensively throughout the Far East, becoming familiar with the vast Pacific territory soon to be caught in the bloody wash of World War II. He learned to fly.

Working with MacArthur, Eisenhower developed a basic respect for him as a brilliant professional soldier. But the difference in their temperaments—MacArthur's towering ego contrasting sharply with Eisenhower's tolerant forthrightness—was too great to permit closeness. Contemplating the end of his tour in the islands, Ike looked forward to a change of bosses as well as of scenery. When war broke out in Europe in 1939—the long-expected war that Fox Conner had bade Ike prepare himself for—Eisenhower, then a lieutenant colonel, put in for a transfer home; he was sure that the U.S. would become involved and was determined not to be left behind again as he had been during World War I.

In General MacArthur's office in Manila, Ike stands by as his chief talks on the phone. Their goal: establishment of a force strong enough to defend the island against Japanese attack. Their target date: 1946, the year the Philippines were to become independent. Plans drawn up by MacArthur and Ike were followed almost exactly when the Japanese attacked—even to the last stand on Bataan.

Facing bonus marchers of 1932 (right), MacArthur wipes perspiration from his face (below), while Ike smokes a cigarette. The demonstrating veterans, unemployed and broke in that depression year, had camped by the thousands near the Capitol to press Congress for action on a two billion dollar war-service bonus bill. MacArthur had been ordered merely to see that they moved from the vicinity of the Capitol building. But as Army Chief of Staff, he personally led the troops, armed with bayoneted rifles and wearing gas masks, that drove the marchers out of Washington and destroyed their camp.

FROM ALL STATES
VETERANS
AMERICA
FIRST IN WASHINGTON
the BONUS
VETERANS
AMERICA

Arriving in Manila, Ike stands respectfully behind MacArthur with other aides and Philippine officials as the general takes a salute. In civilian clothes, both officers saluted with their "boaters" over their hearts.

Major Eisenhower To Be MacArthur's Aide in Philippines

WASHINGTON, Sept. 23 (AP)—Major Dwight B. Eisenhower, aide to General Douglas MacArthur, retiring army chief of staff, left today for a week's visit with relatives at Abilene, Kan., before proceeding to the Philippine Islands.

General MacArthur is to be military adviser to the new Philippine government, and Major Eisenhower will be one of his three aides. The major will join MacArthur in Cheyenne, Wyo., for the trip to the Philippines.

An Associated Press dispatch, announcing Ike's forthcoming departure for the Philippines as one of MacArthur's aides, was mistakenly printed with his middle initial as "B." Throughout his early career Eisenhower was plagued by frequent misspellings of his name.

FROM AN ISLAND ALBUM

Cool in off-duty whites before departing on a Philippine vacation, Ike had his picture taken with Mamie and John (left). John, an early camera bug, caught his father in a moment of relaxation wearing a gaily patterned native kimono; his mother was photographed wearing a Filipino costume, the "terno."

ARMY A.C.

A NEW SKILL, A LAST CEREMONY

"If you see something interesting you can just drop down and look at it, then you soar up again—you can do anything you please."

In 1939, the year the Eisenhowers returned to the United States, student pilot Ike sits under the wing of a Philippine Air Force Stinson Reliant. Standing at his right is one of his instructors. Eisenhower, who loved the air, was judged a "natural" flyer according to Army pilots who saw him in action. In later years Ike occasionally liked to take the controls of planes to ease the boredom of long flights—but drew the line at flying jets.

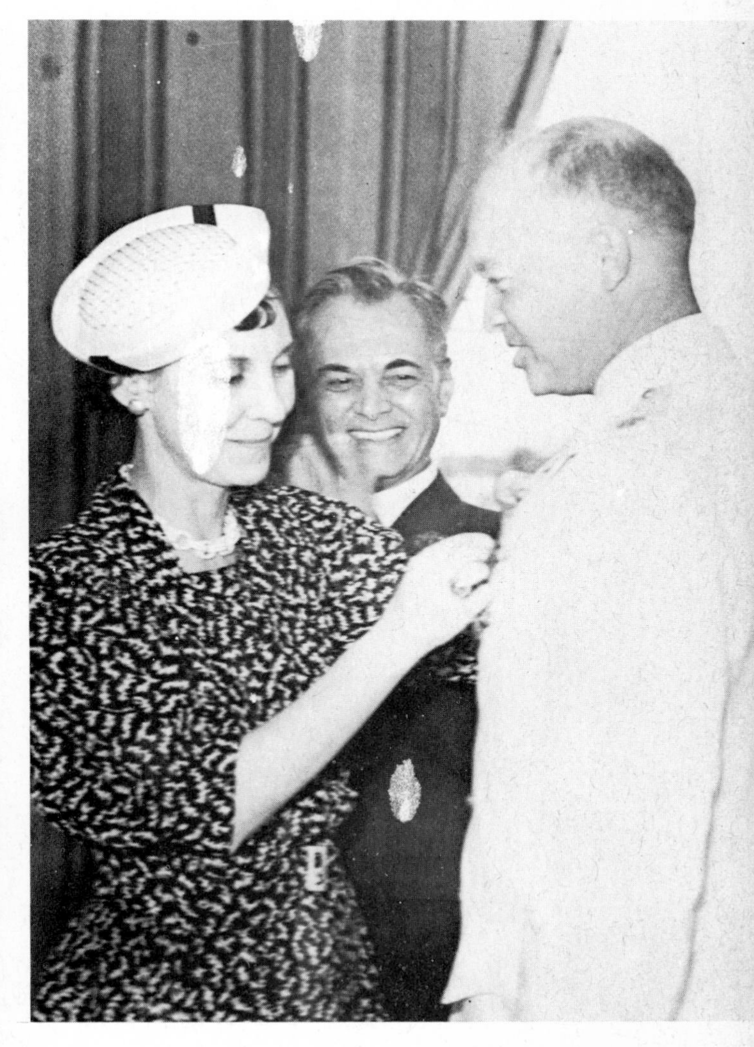

President Manuel Quezon—who tried to persuade Ike to stay in the Philippines—grins as Mamie pins the Philippine government's Distinguished Service Cross on her husband's chest at the end of his tour in the islands.

THE END OF THE BEGINNING

4

Hitler's invasion of Poland in September 1939 plunged the world into six years of global conflict. But for a long time following the outbreak of World War II, the U.S. Army was in many ways a mirror of the complacency that gripped much of the rest of the nation. When Eisenhower returned from the Philippines in January 1940, some two years were still to pass before the United States, in the sudden fury of Pearl Harbor, would be drawn into the fighting. Fortunately, in that twilight of peace, a few key American military leaders were urgently trying to strengthen the nation's defenses against what they felt was the inevitable day of wrath. Dwight Eisenhower was among those who helped make these preparations. On his return from the islands, he was assigned to troop duty at Fort Lewis, Washington—helping to train the new civilian soldiers inducted in America's first peacetime draft; but with his gifts as a staff officer, he was soon promoted to chief of staff of the Third Infantry Division and later of the Ninth Army Corps—an assignment that carried the temporary rank of colonel.

In the late summer of 1941, as German panzers churned across the Ukraine, Congress had extended the draft—by the slender margin of one House vote—and the Army had grown to a record peacetime strength of 1,500,000 men. To help train this burgeoning force for combat, the Army held the biggest peacetime exercises in its history in September of 1941—the Louisiana maneuvers. These war games enhanced Eisenhower's growing reputation and brought him his first glimmers of public recognition. The sham battle involved some 400,000 troops in two armies commanded by Lieutenant Generals Walter Krueger and Ben Lear. For Ike it was a crucial test; he was given a key job as chief of staff for Krueger's Third Army, with the responsibility of planning strategy for the maneuvers. His primary problem was to use the Third Army's defensive power to stop the "enemy" Second Army, which had a superior armored striking force.

As the maneuvers unfolded, Krueger's Third Army scored decisive victories. Ike got credit as the architect of the triumph and was praised in a syndicated newspaper column by Drew Pearson and Robert S. Allen; they wrote that it was "Colonel Eisenhower. . .who conceived and directed the strategy that routed the Second Army," adding that Krueger's

Shortly before the invasion of North Africa, Ike confers with the two members of his staff who were closest to him, Generals Walter Bedell Smith (left) and Mark W. Clark. As Chief of Staff, Bedell Smith has often been called Eisenhower's most inspired appointment. Ike described him as "a godsend —a master of detail with a clear comprehension of main issues." Following the War, Bedell Smith held various important government posts: Ambassador to Russia, Director of the CIA and Undersecretary of State in Eisenhower's first term as President.

chief of staff "has a steel-trap mind plus unusual physical vigor. . . ." Official recognition was also swift: shortly after the maneuvers Ike was given another temporary promotion—his brigadier general's star.

With the bombing of Pearl Harbor on December 7, Eisenhower was ordered to Washington by George C. Marshall, then Army Chief of Staff. His first assignment was in the Office of War Plans, where he helped formulate the strategy the United States was to follow throughout the War; at a time when the Allies' fortunes were at their lowest ebb, he was already planning for the eventual invasion of France. Eisenhower made such an impression on Marshall that in the spring of 1942 he was sent to England to devise a master plan for a unified command of American forces in Europe. Among his recommendations was the appointment of a single commander to be in overall charge of ground, air and naval operations; for that key post he suggested his old classmate General Joseph T. McNarney.

But it was not McNarney who got the job—it was Eisenhower. As Commanding General, European Theater of Operations, he flew to London in late June of 1942 to assume the tremendous responsibilities that he was to carry until the War ended. Almost overnight he became one of the most important and famous men alive.

Eisenhower quickly demonstrated his flair for organization, assembling a staff that included some of the Army's most brilliant officers. When it was decided to invade French North Africa as a prelude to attack on Europe, the Allied Combined Chiefs of Staff named Ike Allied commander in chief—in charge of "Operation Torch," the code name for the North African invasion plan. Only four months later, in early November, he directed the "Torch" landings from new headquarters in Gibraltar. The assaults were spectacularly successful, but the North African adventure involved political as well as military battles, and from these Eisenhower did not always escape unscathed.

Prior to the invasion, Ike and his advisers had hoped to avoid resistance from the German-dominated Vichy French, who governed Northwest Africa, by appointing French General Henri Giraud to take charge of political affairs after the invasion. It was believed that Giraud had great influence with French officers in the Vichy camp—although, as a prisoner-of-war, captured before the fall of France, he had never acknowledged Vichy. It was hoped that Giraud could prevail upon his countrymen to forswear their oaths to Vichy and join the Allies. But Giraud, spirited out of France in a submarine after escaping from the Germans and secretly brought to Ike's headquarters before the invasion, insisted that he could accept no lesser role than the command of the entire Allied expedition. Only after long negotiations that tested Ike's carefully hoarded supply of patience, did Giraud agree to settle for command of the French forces fighting alongside the Allies. Unfortunately, when he called upon his brother-officers serving Vichy to cease resisting the Allied invasion forces, he proved to be a leader without a following; in most cases, the Vichy French officers in Africa simply ignored him.

As the Allies established beachheads, Eisenhower began searching for another leader who could unify the French. By luck, during the invasion of Algiers, his troops had captured Admiral Jean Darlan, commander-in-chief of all Vichy French forces, and deputy to Marshal Henri Pétain, the World War I hero who headed the Vichy Government. The captive Darlan agreed to cooperate with the Allies. Eisenhower took a calculated political risk by putting him—an avowed traitor but a skillful politician—in charge of the French government apparatus in North

frica. But he felt the risk was justified by the opportunity offered of reducing French resistance and saving lives. oth the British and the U.S. governments supported his ction (as did Giraud), but dealing with a collaborator rought Eisenhower the most severe criticism he was to uffer during the entire War. The Darlan arrangement vorked well enough until, on Christmas Eve, 1942, Daran was assassinated by a young French student. Once nore Ike had to find a French leader. For lack of anyone lse with the required stature the French agreed on Giaud as a replacement for Darlan, despite the fact that hey had previously rejected him.

Meanwhile, following the successful landings, the military campaign in North Africa moved swiftly. In October, General Sir Bernard Montgomery's British Eighth Army had defeated the Axis forces at El Alamein in Egypt and sent them fleeing westward toward Tunisia; the stage was being set for the entrapment of all Axis forces in North Africa as Allied troops simultaneously hit the enemy from the west. As the Germans suffered their first major setbacks of the War, Eisenhower and his political superiors in the Allied camp could at last begin to feel that the tide had turned—that, as Prime Minister Winston Churchill put it, the end of the War had begun.

Through the smoke of simulated battle during the Louisiana maneuvers, cavalrymen of the Third Army trot past an abandoned "enemy" tank. The horses gave way to tanks and jeeps after Pearl Harbor, and U.S. cavalry units were all mechanized.

AFTERMATH

U.S. Navy planes burn on Ford Island (below) in Pearl Harbor after the Japanese attack on December 7, 1941, brought the War to America. At the time the Japanese bombs fell on Hawaii, Ike was stationed at Fort Sam Houston in Texas. Summoned to Washington (left), he replaced Brigadier General Leonard T. Gerow as Chief of War Plans.

OF INFAMY

General George C. Marshall, Army Chief of Staff at the time of Pearl Harbor, personally ordered Eisenhower to come to Washington only five days after the Japanese attack. Convinced that America could not stay out of the fighting, Marshall had been carefully screening officers he could count on to help run the War. Ike was one of his first choices.

SUDDEN FAME IN A NEW ROLE: SOLDIER-STATESMAN

As a commander of American forces in Europe, Eisenhower was thrust into a new role—that of the soldier-statesman. In the twilight zone of military and political affairs, he had to command his country's forces and those of the Allies—but he also had to win over Allied politicians. From the time he arrived in Great Britain he was confronted by the problems raised by another soldier-statesman—General Charles de Gaulle. Based in London as head of an ad hoc Free French "government," De Gaulle was a standard-bearer for ordinary Frenchmen living under the Nazi occupation. But because De Gaulle's headquarters security was notoriously bad, it was American-British policy not to let the Frenchman know anything about the North African invasion plans for fear they would be leaked to the enemy. De Gaulle also posed another problem: although he was popular with the French civilian populace, he was unpopular with the Vichy government's military forces. The Allies believed that if he were allowed to take part in the invasion of North Africa his presence would stiffen the resistance of Vichy troops there; at the same time they hoped he would remain to unify all of the French people once the collaborationist Vichy government had been discredited by Allied victories in North Africa and the continent of Europe.

Newly appointed as commander of American forces in the European theater—and suddenly a celebrity—Ike smiles for news photographers soon after his arrival in his London headquarters.

In a historic first meeting witnessed by Admiral Harold Stark (wearing glasses), U.S. Naval commander in Europe, Eisenhower and Free French General Charles de Gaulle shake hands in London.

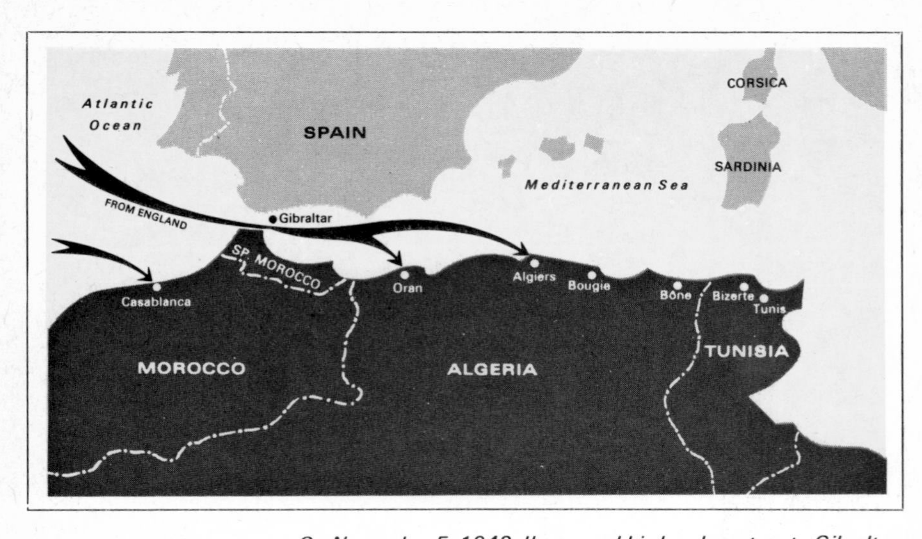

On November 5, 1942, Ike moved his headquarters to Gibraltar, and three days later some 300,000 British, U.S. and Free French troops under his command invaded French North Africa. Targets were Casablanca, Oran and Algiers as shown on the map above. The assault was primarily made up of U.S. troops; the Allies wanted to give it as American a character as possible: for one thing, French reaction to British shelling of their fleet in Oran harbor in 1940 was still bitter. U.S. forces, displaying the Stars and Stripes for identification, met no French opposition as they landed just east of Algiers (right). There was stiff resistance by the French at Oran and Casablanca, but the entire area west of Algiers was in Allied hands within three days after the landing.

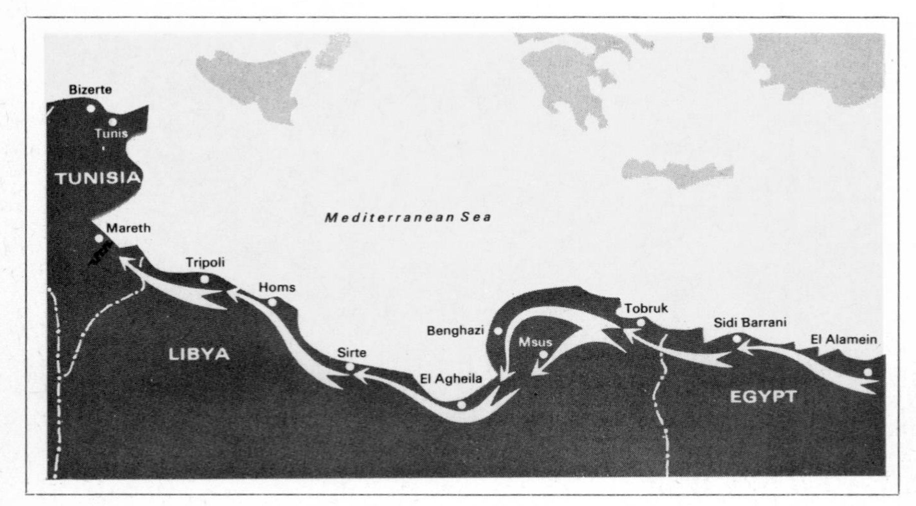

In a climactic action that was timed to support the Allied landing, General Bernard Montgomery's British Eighth Army broke out of El Alamein, 65 miles west of Alexandria, on October 25 and began driving German General Erwin Rommel's vaunted Afrika Korps to the west along the path shown on the map above. With Montgomery advancing westward and Eisenhower pushing eastward toward Tunisia, the Allies aimed to squeeze the German and Italian forces in a nutcracker. At right, British infantrymen capture a German tank crew at bayonet point during the fierce desert fighting, which was the last of its kind in World War II.

K-27-12

With General Mark Clark as witness, Ike lays down the law to Admiral Jean Darlan, the captured Vichy French leader whom Eisenhower had gotten the Allies to recognize as de facto head of the French Government in North Africa. Darlan, widely regarded as untrustworthy, nevertheless became the key to French cooperation with the Allies in North Africa. The more reliable General Henri Giraud, shown at far right riding with Ike after the landings, was ignored by local French commanders, and the capture of Darlan, who (by chance) was visiting a sick son in Algiers when the Allies landed, was a godsend; as deputy to Marshal Henri Petain, head of the Vichy Government, Darlan was the only man whose orders most French officers serving in North Africa would obey.

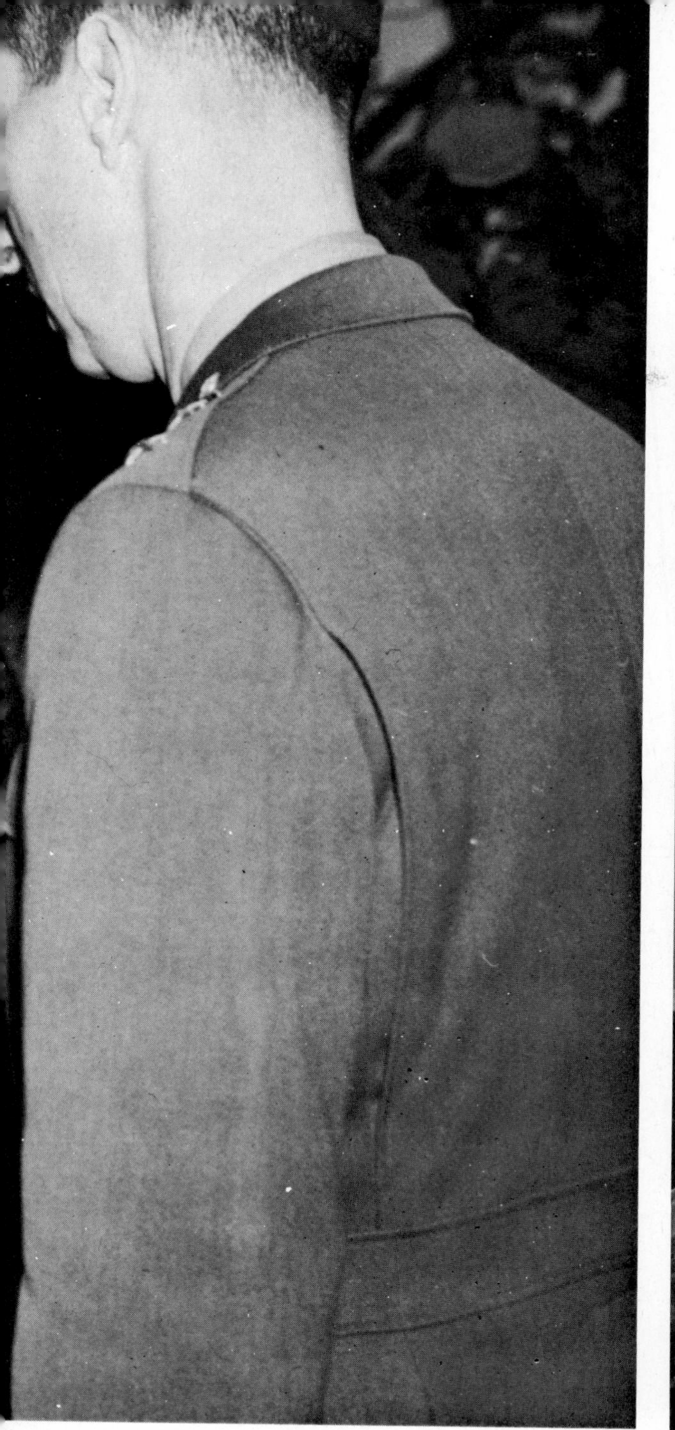

In naval uniform, Admiral Darlan reviews a parade in Vichy, standing between the cane-carrying Marshal Henri Petain and Premier Pierre Laval. After the War, Petain and Laval were tried for treason by the new French Government. The picture at left was taken shortly before Darlan, commander-in-chief of all Vichy armed forces under Petain, was captured by the Allies.

CARRYING "TORCH" TO VICTORY—AND BEYOND

The seizure of the main ports along the North African coast gave the Allies the initial objective of Operation Torch—to stop the Axis from using the ports for submarine bases. With this achieved, Ike turned to the primary purpose of his mission—to cooperate with General Sir Harold Alexander's British forces (including Montgomery's Eighth Army, some 1,200 miles distant in the Western Desert), in the destruction of Axis troops in North Africa.

Hoping to score a quick victory by cutting the enemy's lines of communication with Europe, Ike boldly ordered a charge eastward toward the Axis stronghold at Tunis, some 400 miles from Algiers, without taking time to build up supplies and reinforcements for the drive. It was a gamble but it seemed to have a good chance of succeeding, although the Germans and Italians were rapidly reinforcing their armies in Tunis.

Meanwhile, the British Eighth Army under Montgomery continued its westward pursuit of the enemy. But before the Americans and British could link up, the weather in northern Algeria and Tunis turned bad, and Ike's offensive bogged down—mainly from lack of motor transport and close-up air support.

As the attack stalled, Eisenhower made a personal trip to the front to try to get it moving again. But he soon recognized that the torrential winter rains and the deep, gluelike mud they produced made fighting impossible; there was no choice except to dig in and wait until spring. Barely had he made this bitter decision when he received the news that Admiral Darlan had been assassinated in Algiers. On Christmas Eve Ike began a 30-hour nonstop drive back to his Algiers headquarters to deal with this latest crisis in French affairs. For months he had been working at a punishing pace, and the long trip pushed him over the brink of endurance; he came down with a severe attack of flu on Christmas Day and was in bed for four days, too sick to move (it was the only time he was ill during the entire War).

Soon after his recovery, however, things started taking a turn for the better. The political situation was stabilized when French officials agreed that General Giraud, whose leadership they had once rejected, was the

In a widely publicized show of Allied unity, President Roosevelt and Prime Minister Churchill were photographed at Casablanca with rival Free French Generals Charles de Gaulle (second from right) and Henri Giraud (left). The American and British leaders were hopeful that the two stubborn Frenchmen—each claiming to represent French resistance—could be reconciled. De Gaulle and Giraud exchanged grudging handshakes and sat with F.D.R. and Churchill for the press cameras, but the reconciliation was short-lived; De Gaulle never really accepted it.

only logical successor to Darlan. This placed Giraud in rivalry with De Gaulle for leadership of the Free French movement, but their differences were reconciled, for the moment at least, during the meeting between Churchill and Roosevelt at the North African town of Casablanca in January—a conference held on freshly reconquered soil to dramatize the new direction of the War.

Eisenhower took little part in these political moves. In the single day he was able to spend at the conference he barely had a chance to participate in the decision to invade Sicily and Italy following the end of the North African campaign. Of more immediate concern to Eisenhower was another decision of the Allied high command: the victorious British Eighth Army was to be placed under his control. He found this "extraordinarily pleasing" because it assured complete unity of action in the North African theater under a single commander—a set-up he had always favored. To go with his new status, Ike got his fourth star and became a full general.

On February 12, the day after Ike's promotion came through, he made one of his frequent inspection tours of the front. Allied intelligence had warned that the enemy was preparing an offensive, and Eisenhower was disturbed to find that his troops were complacent; he complained of "unconscionable delay" in the preparation of defenses for their positions. That same day, before corrective measures could be taken, the enemy launched a powerful attack. In the ensuing battle around the notorious Kasserine Pass, green American troops reeled back from their weakly fortified lines. But by the 22nd the Axis drive had been halted, and Ike ordered a counterattack that forced the enemy to retreat. On March 20, General Montgomery's Eighth Army boldly attacked German fortifications near Mareth and flanked the "Mareth Line" in a brilliant surprise maneuver that forced a general enemy withdrawal behind a shortened line closer to Tunis. The Germans no longer stood between Montgomery's men and Ike's, and for the first time all Allied troops in North Africa were linked in a single line of battle, poised for the kill. The final assault on Tunis began on May 5 and moved so swiftly that the campaign for North Africa was over in a little more than a week.

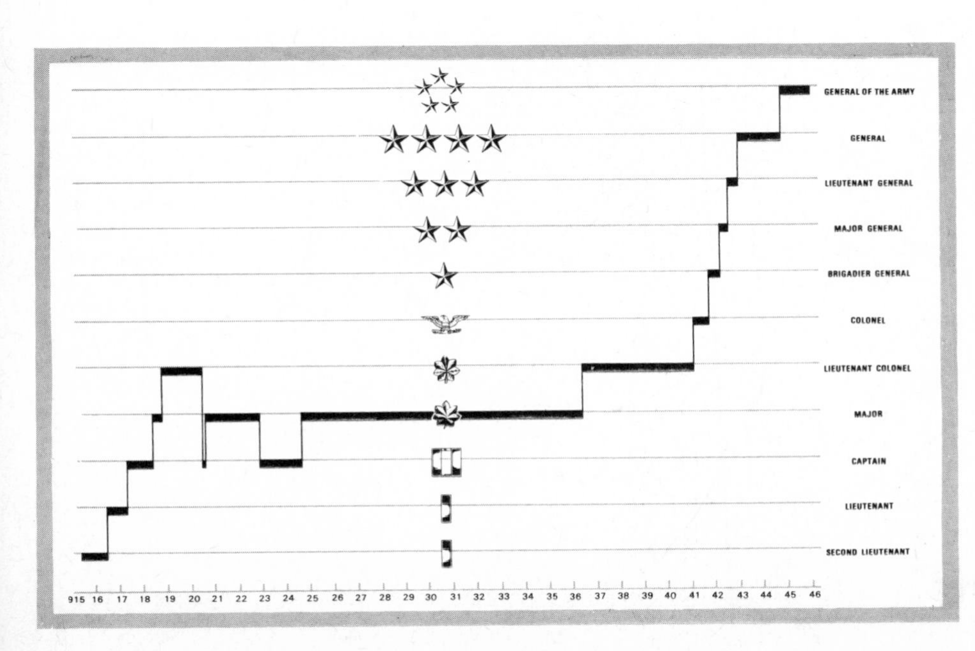

The heavy horizontal lines on the chart at left show Ike's promotions and length of time in various ranks. At the end of World War I he had reached the temporary rank of lieutenant colonel, but reverted to his permanent rank of captain; after three days he was promoted to the temporary grade of major, but in an economy drive two years later he was once more reduced to a captain; there were 12 long years when he was stuck as a major. In World War II his rise was phenomenal; he became a five-star general on December 15, 1944—the day before the Battle of the Bulge.

THE COUP DE GRACE IN TUNISIA

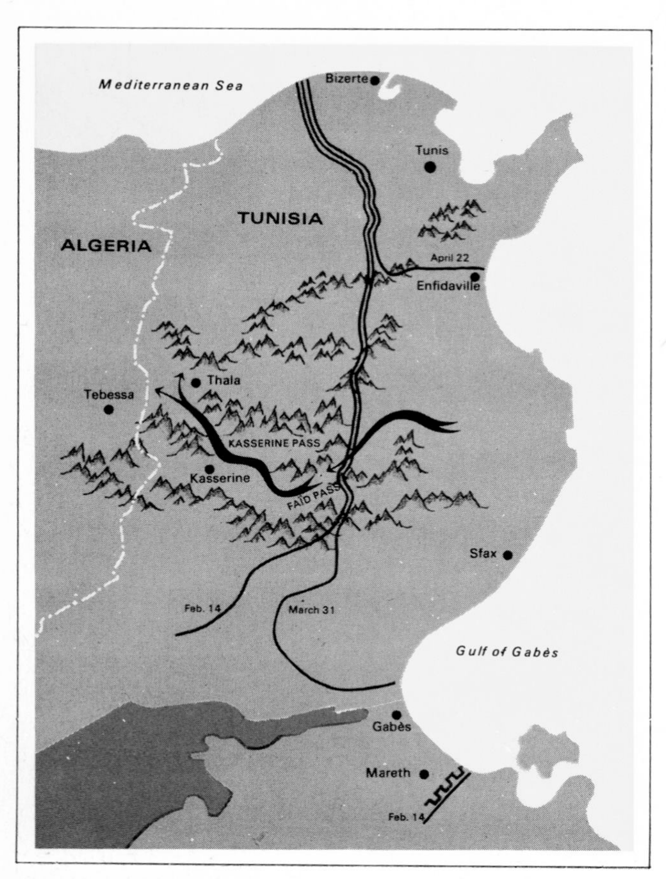

As the 1943 campaign in North Africa approached its climax, Allied troops were in the positions indicated on the map at left by the lines dated February 14: Ike's forces were holding a line from a point west of Bizerte through the passes of the Atlas Mountains; Montgomery's British faced the enemy at the Mareth Line (lower right). Following a serious threat from Axis forces attacking in February through the Kasserine Pass, the Allies pushed the enemy back to the line dated March 31. Meanwhile, Montgomery had outflanked the Mareth Line and linked up with other Allied forces to form a continuous line. By April 22, thrusting toward Tunis on the right side of their line and holding their positions on the left side, the Allies had jammed the Germans and Italians into the confined area between Bizerte and Enfidaville—virtually ending the campaign. The coup de grâce came on May 13, and in the last week of the campaign alone the prisoner bag reached an awesome—and unwieldy—total of 240,000.

"They never taught me in General Staff and Command School what to do with a quarter-million prisoners."

For his leadership of American troops in the victorious battle for Tunisia, as commander of the U.S. II Corps, General George Patton (above) receives his third star from Ike.

American soldiers add to a mountain of helmets and other military equipment taken from captured members of the once-proud Afrika Korps in the battle for Tunisia.

THE STROKES THAT FINISHED ITALY

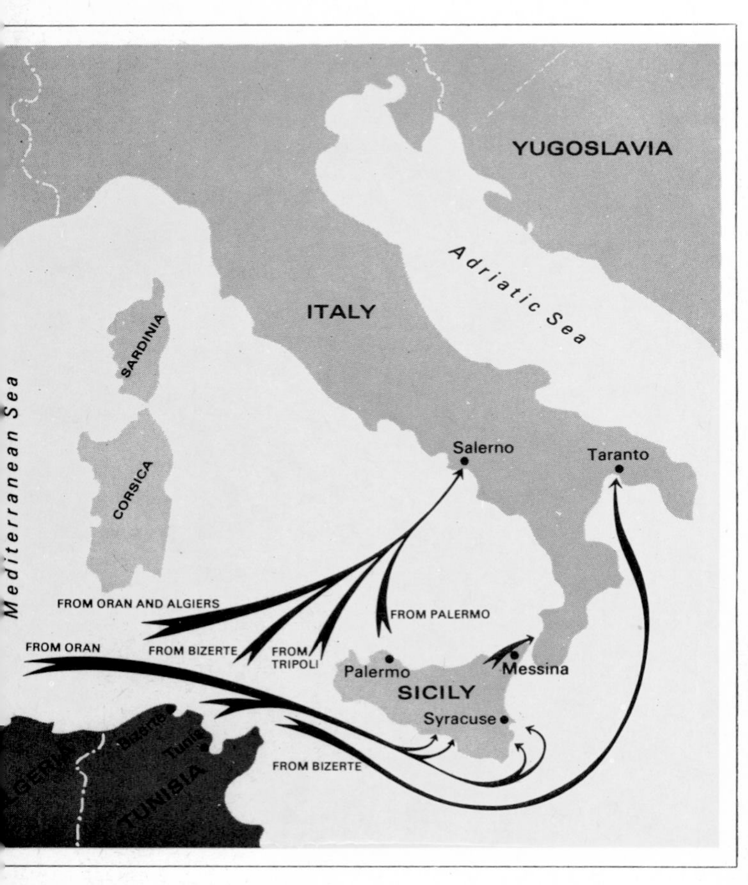

On July 10, two months after the end of the fighting in North Africa, Allied troops jumped off for landings in Sicily, heading for the points indicated by lower arrows on the map above. Within 38 days the island fell, and on September 9, Eisenhower's forces invaded the Italian mainland, landing at Salerno and Taranto. The Italian government surrendered the day before the attack on the mainland, but the Germans fought on in Italy.

Meeting with Allied leaders in his Algiers headquarters after the victory at Tunis, Eisenhower helps plan the forthcoming Italian campaign. Seated with him at the table are Prime Minister Churchill and General Marshall; in a semicircle around them, left to right, are British Foreign Minister Sir Anthony Eden; General Sir Alan Brooke, Chief of the British Imperial General Staff; Air Chief Marshal Sir Arthur Tedder of the RAF, Commander in Chief of Allied Air Forces; the Royal Navy's Admiral Sir Andrew Cunningham, Commander in Chief of Allied Naval Forces; General Sir Harold Alexander, Ike's deputy commander; and General Sir Bernard Montgomery, Commander of the British Eighth Army.

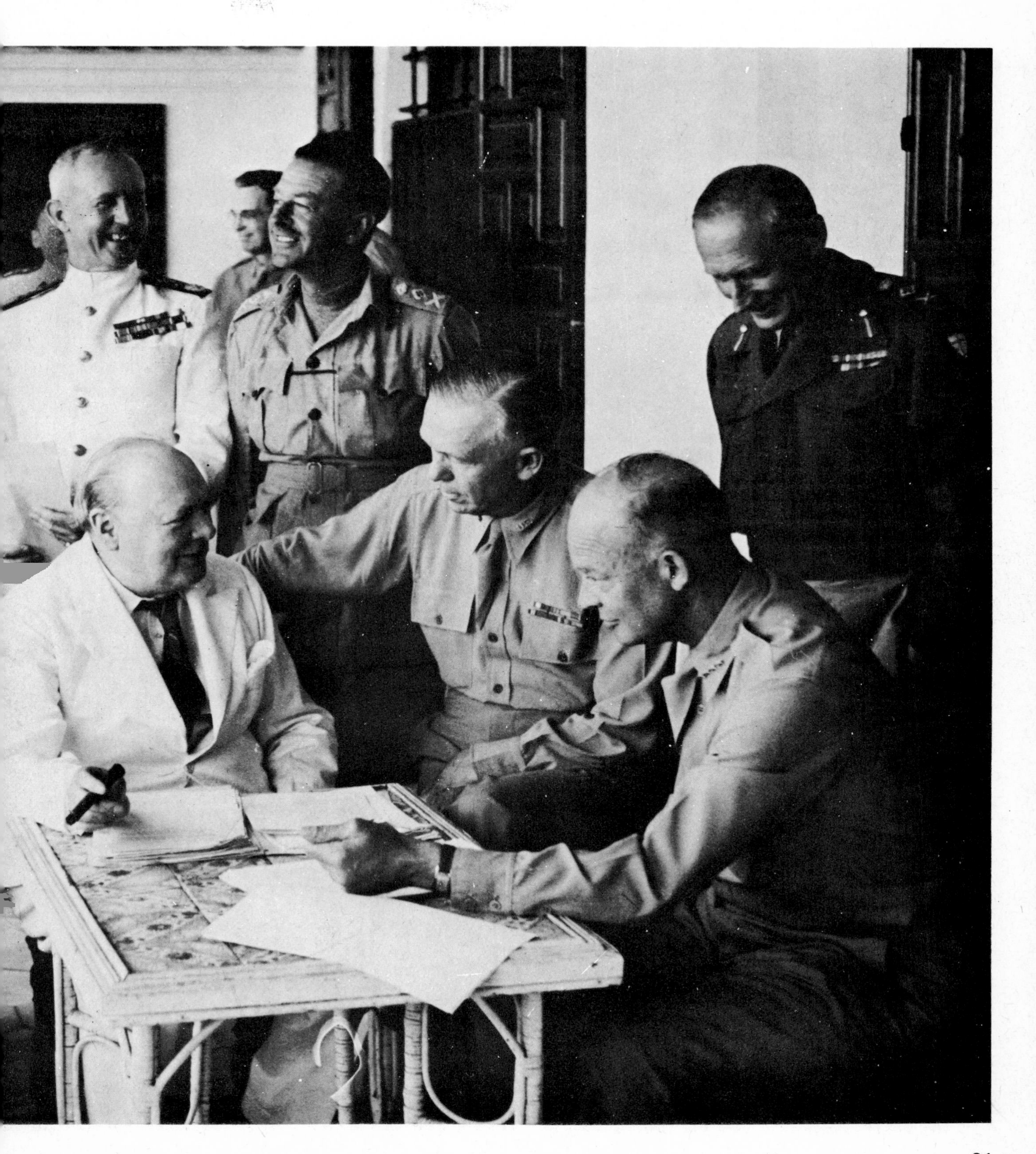

Newspapers with banner headlines announcing the invasion of France by an Allied armada are eagerly snapped up at a Chicago newsstand early on June 6, 1944. All over the nation the long-awaited news brought the mingled hope, elation and anxiety that can be seen in the face of the woman at right.

ASSAULT, PURSUIT, VICTORY

5

By the end of 1943, a war-torn world lived in day-to-day anticipation of one clarion word: invasion. It meant assault on the Continent, the Second Front that the Soviets had so long agitated for, liberation, victory. Eisenhower's masterly handling of the tangled challenges—political as well as military—of Operation Torch made him an almost automatic choice to lead the grand onslaught across the Channel, code-named Operation Overlord. Shortly after Christmas, 1943, Ike moved his headquarters back to England to oversee the buildup. Soon men and materials were pouring into Great Britain in unprecedented, lavish profusion. The tonnage was so great, according to one contemporary joke, that only the barrage balloons—small blimps moored to the ground by heavy cables designed to hamper attacking aircraft—were keeping the British Isles afloat.

The invasion was scheduled for June 5, but the worst weather in 20 years forced a postponement. Though the meteorologists predicted a brief break in the storm in 24 hours, the uncertainties of weather forecasting led Ike onto the horns of the cruelest dilemma he was to face throughout the War. The troops were ready to go—some were already on board ships. If he delayed, the tides would not be right again for two weeks—plenty of time for the Nazis to pierce the screens of secrecy shielding the assault. Even so, for security reasons the troops would have to be kept penned up in their camps or aboard their ships. In a fortnight's waiting, it would be all too easy for them to grow restive and lose the keen edge of their excitement and anticipation. But if he proceeded at once and the weather did not break, the invasion would end in disaster. Ike spent an agonizing night weighing all of the possibilities. Then he decided to gamble on a change in the weather. "Well, we'll go," he said, unleashing a striking force of some 1,000,000 men, 11,000 planes and 4,000 ships—the mightiest armada in the history of war.

Ike accompanies a bowler-hatted Prime Minister Churchill (facing away from the camera) on a preinvasion inspection visit to a supply depot. The spit-and-polish appearance of the American soldier at right was the invasion's first casualty.

Holding field glasses as he waits for tank gunnery practice to begin, Ike observes a U.S. armored unit drill at a tank range in England in February 1944. Beside him, smoking a pipe, is Air Chief Marshal Sir Arthur Tedder.

Watching the tank practice firing, old tanker Eisenhower registers (from left, below) anticipation, annoyance, concern, absorption, elation—and finally—approval.

INVASION EVE

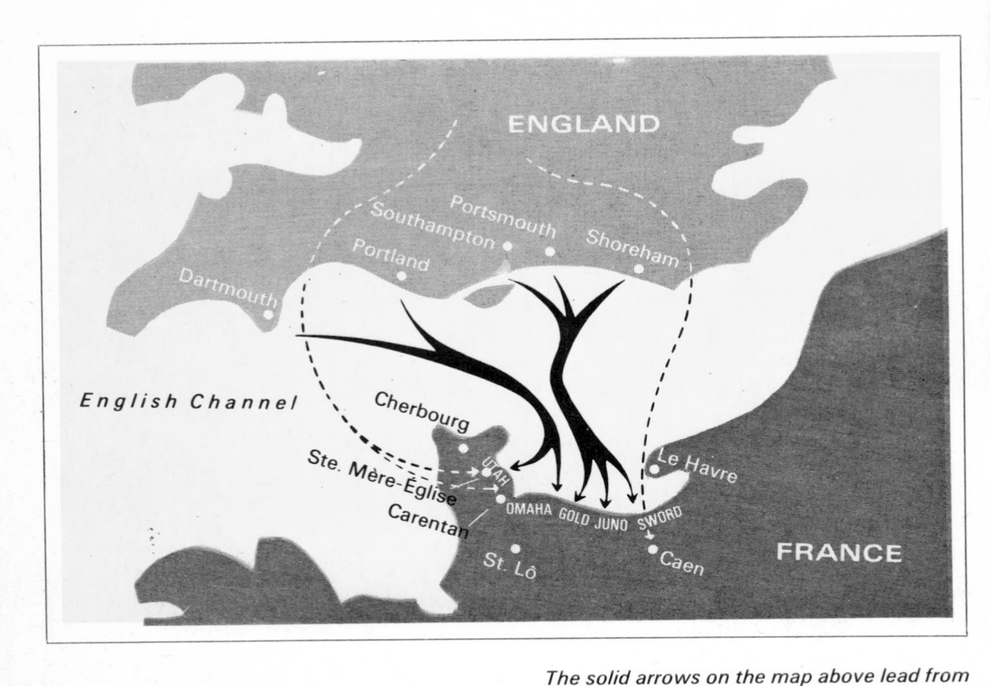

The solid arrows on the map above lead from the British embarkation ports used by the invasion forces to the five Normandy beaches (code-named in capitals) that the troops assaulted on D-Day. Curved dotted arrows represent the air routes and landing points of Allied airborne troops. Their mission: to block bridges and causeways leading to the beachheads and prevent the enemy from bringing up reinforcements.

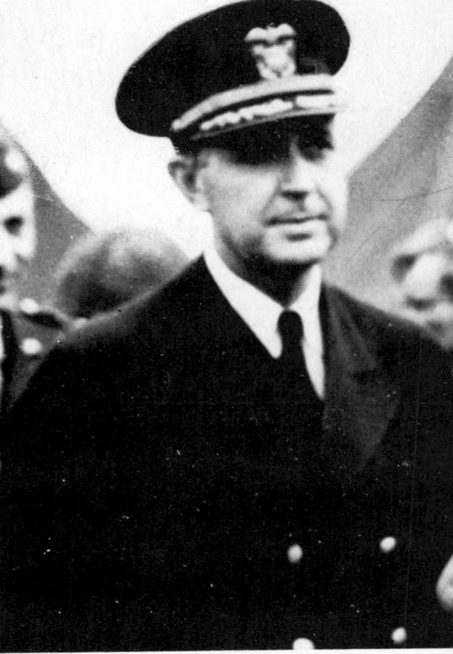

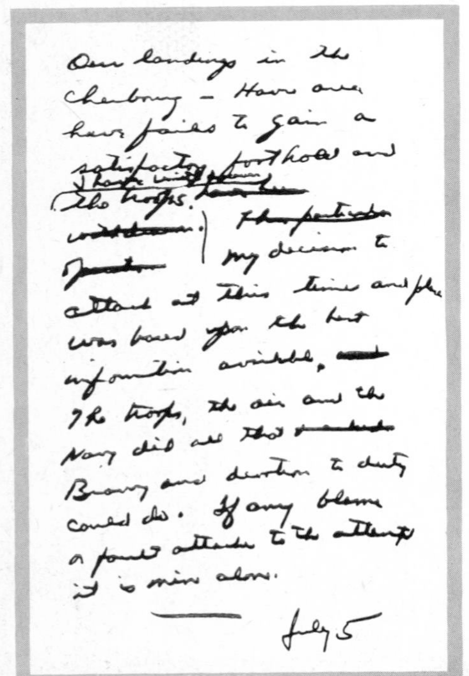

Our landings in the
Cherbourg – Havre area
have failed to gain a
satisfactory foothold and
~~I have withdrawn~~
the troops. ~~have been~~
~~withdrawn.~~ | ~~This particular~~
~~operation~~ | My decision to
attack at this time and place
was based upon the best
information available, ~~and~~
The troops, the air and the
Navy did all that ~~human~~
Bravery and devotion to duty
could do. If any blame
or fault attaches to the attempt
it is mine alone.

July 5

Assailed by secret doubts—which he carefully concealed from those around him—about the invasion's chances, Eisenhower scratched off the note at left, taking upon himself the entire blame for possible failure. He dated it a month ahead and stuffed it in his wallet.

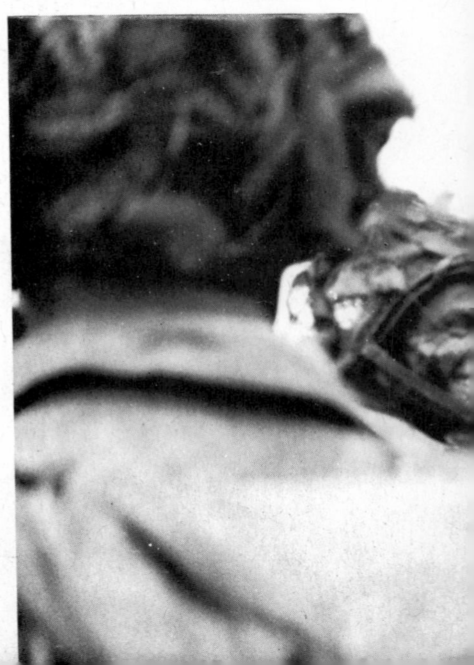

The night before D-Day, Ike chats and jokes with members of the U.S. 101st Airborne Division, camouflaged in preparation for their jump behind enemy lines. At left in the center panel is Eisenhower's naval aide, Commander Harry Butcher. Many men of the 101st, hampered by poor weather, darkness and enemy ground fire, landed from eight to 20 miles off target. But by noon the next day the paratroopers had made contact with infantrymen of General J. Lawton Collins' VII Corps, the conquerors of Utah Beach.

23

American infantrymen charge down the ramp of a landing craft and plunge through shallow waves onto bitterly defended Omaha Beach (bottom). Approaching the shore, they take cover among heavy timber obstacles (top) erected by the Germans as part of their effort to build a beach defense system.

FIRST LOOK AT LIBERATED EUROPE

On D-Day Plus One (June 7, 1944) Ike joins two of his top commanders, British Admiral Sir Bertram Ramsey (left) and General Montgomery, aboard the destroyer HMS Apollo off Omaha Beach. It was at this landing point the stiffest resistance was met; although the enemy had been dislodged by the American 1st and 29th Divisions, the beachhead was still being shelled as Ike watched from the Apollo.

Seen at left in the rear of a command car, Eisenhower accompanies General Marshall (seated beside him) and General Courtney Hodges (wearing helmet) on a tour of newly won territory five days after the Normandy landings. Marshall had come from Washington with Admiral Ernest King and General Henry (Hap) Arnold, Army Air Force Chief, to see for themselves how the invasion was going.

In the pictures at right, taken during the critical days following the landings, Ike busily guides his superiors (who had come to view a corner of liberated France) around the beachhead and visits his own subordinates: **1** *While curious GIs watch, Eisenhower washes off beachhead grime between inspection tours with the top brass;* **2** *Aboard an amphibious "duck," Eisenhower (wearing sunglasses) surveys the beach with his high-ranking guests —General Marshall (far left) and Admiral Ernest King, U.S. Chief of Naval Operations (behind driver) and their staffs;* **3** *Eyes cocked up at the Allied aircraft that dominated the beachhead, Admiral King, Generals Marshall, Hap Arnold and Ike clamber into a "duck";* **4** *With Generals Omar Bradley and Courtney Hodges, Ike briefs King George VI after the British monarch's arrival in Normandy;* **5** *Eisenhower and Air Chief Marshall Tedder call on the top Allied ground commander, General Montgomery, in his highly individual battle dress, at Monty's headquarters.*

1

2

3

4

5

BREAKOUT: THE DRIVE TO THE RHINE

Their beachhead in France secured and their supplies pouring in, the Allies broke out of Normandy on July 25. Following the breakout, Ike planned to advance on a broad front, aiming to destroy the enemy and his capacity to make war, rather than merely to take ground or capture prisoners. This contrasted sharply with a strategy favored by General Montgomery, and the dispute led to friction between him and Ike. The Montgomery plan called for a "concentrated thrust" by British troops (under Monty) through the Low Countries toward the vital industrial area of the Ruhr, and on to Berlin *(see maps at right)*. In Montgomery's view, this scheme had one cardinal virtue: the thrust at Germany's industrial heart would quickly win the War. Ike and his staff rejected Montgomery's proposal. Their argument: the plan was too restricted to succeed; the "thrust" would outrun supplies and run the risk of being cut off inside Germany; meanwhile the rest of the front, relegated to a containment role and starved of supplies, would have to remain stationary and would, ran Ike's reasoning, be exposed to dangerous enemy attacks. Eisenhower decreed a strategy of multiple coordinate drives on a broad front with secure flanks.

As these decisions were reached, the Germans continued to fall back toward the Seine, suffering enormous losses in both men and materials. A particularly fierce battle was fought at Falaise, 150 miles west of Paris, as the enemy struggled desperately against encirclement. Ike described the Falaise "pocket" as "one of the greatest 'killing grounds' of any of the war areas. Roads, highways and fields were so choked with destroyed equipment and with dead men and animals that passage through the area was extremely difficult. . . . It was literally possible to walk for hundreds of yards at a time, stepping on nothing but dead and decaying flesh."

When the surviving Germans retreated across the Seine, Ike was suddenly confronted with a new and urgent political problem: what to do about Paris? The Allies had taken pains to avoid bombing the French capital, and tried to force the Nazis to surrender it without

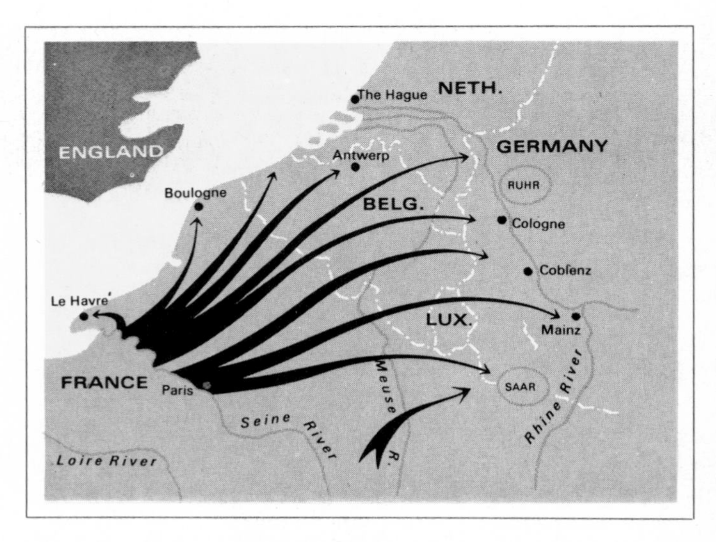

Thrusting out from the Normandy beachhead, the arrows on the map above diagram the strategy followed by the armies under Eisenhower in his "broadfront" plan. This scheme eventually spread the armies out along the entire western border of Germany.

The "concentrated thrust" (large arrow) advocated by Montgomery (and turned down by Ike) called for a narrow probing drive toward the Ruhr by three armies. In concept, it was a massive flanking maneuver designed to follow the shortest distance between the Channel Coast and Berlin. Remaining forces (small arrow) would have had the formidable task of protecting the flank of the operation.

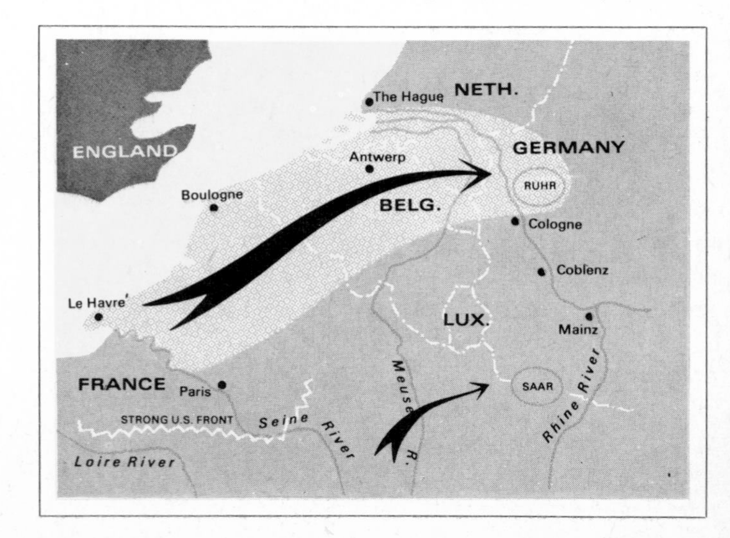

On August 29, 1944, the 28th Division, scrubbed and resplendent with shining brass and loaded weapons, marches down the Champs Elysées (left). The division band played "Khaki Bill"; once through Paris, the troops resumed their attack on the enemy.

damage by cutting it off and surrounding it. In fact, Ike did not want Paris to capitulate at that time; as a military objective, he felt it was valueless. He preferred to keep pressing the retreating Germans and maintain the impetus of the advance; taking Paris would, he was convinced, only slow it down.

However, his hand was forced when the Free French inside the city rose against their German masters and it became necessary to go to their support. The Germans threatened to bomb the city if the uprising continued. After frantic conferences, the Allied command arranged for the French Second Armored Division to liberate the City of Light from Nazi occupation. Unfortunately, the Second Armored stopped so often to celebrate its mission that General Bradley became impatient and ordered the U.S. Fourth Armored Division "to slam on in and take the liberation." This move so distressed the Second Armored that, according to one account, they mounted their Sherman tanks and "burned up their treads on the brick roads" getting to Paris ahead of the Americans.

The formal surrender took place on August 25, touching off celebrations so exuberant and prolonged that a week later the Second Armored still had not left Paris, and its tanks had to be routed out of alleys and backstreets before the advance could be resumed.

Meanwhile, De Gaulle had taken charge of the city, and he asked Ike for two divisions for a show of strength so that he could establish his position and preserve order. Eisenhower pointed out that he could not spare his troops for any length of time, but he would let De Gaulle take their salute as they marched through Paris on their way to the front, then near the city's eastern outskirts. He declined to join De Gaulle on the reviewing stand, but promised to send General Bradley in his place.

Following the liberation of Paris, the offensive swept on, and by winter the fighting had moved into Germany, where the Allies' lines were so extended that often they stretched dangerously thin. In December, the Germans struck back, gambling on a quick knockout punch to turn defeat into victory. Ironically, the German counter-offensive—which became the Battle of the Bulge—began the day after Ike received his fifth star, making him General of the Army. He was reminded that the day after he got his fourth star his troops suffered a similar setback at the Kasserine Pass in North Africa. It was a coincidence that led him to express mock gratitude that he could receive no more stars.

The German counterattack slashed through the Ardennes Forest on the Belgian-German border on December 16. The Nazis took advantage of a spell of bad weather that made aerial reconnaissance impossible and gave them the advantage of almost total surprise. Swiftly penetrating the thin Allied defensive crust in the Ardennes Forest of Belgium, German tanks thrust swiftly westward; so rapid was their advance (35 miles in the first three days) that they overran rear-area headquarters and cut off American units in St. Vith and Bastogne, a key road junction. Their aim: to seize the bridges over the Meuse River and drive on through to Antwerp, the major Allied supply port for northern Europe. It was a bold move—but it soon revealed the Germans' weaknesses, particularly in logistics. Shortages of fuel for their tanks and trucks and lack of food, sleep and ammunition slowed the German offensive within a week; vigorous Allied attacks against their extended flanks and the heroic resistance offered by the beleaguered troops in Bastogne effectively stopped the drive in its tracks. For Hitler, the price of his last-ditch offensive was high: in the Battle of the Bulge, he lost his last large well-organized, well-trained and well-equipped armored formations on the Western Front.

Though the Germans penetrated the Allied lines some 50 miles before they were halted, at no time did Ike feel that his position was seriously threatened; later he expressed surprise at the furor the attack had caused at home. In early January he resumed his advance, and within two weeks all of the German gains had been wiped out. Under hammering Allied blows, the enemy fell back toward the Rhine, the last great natural barrier protecting the essential industry of the Ruhr valley.

BEYOND THE RIVER BARRIER

On March 7, 1945, the American III Corps reached the Rhine River, appearing so suddenly that the Germans had no time to blow up the Ludendorff Bridge at Remagen, the last remaining crossing. Although the Americans knew the bridge was loaded with demolition charges, a detachment from the Ninth Armored Division clattered across and seized the eastern approaches. Only then did the panicky Germans try to detonate their demolition charges. One charge went off, causing some damage, but the bridge remained largely intact. Ike had expected a time-consuming delay before he could cross the flood-swollen river farther north with assault boats; now, with the Remagen bridge unexpectedly in Allied hands, he ordered five divisions to cross it immediately, giving him a bridgehead on the east bank and shortening the War by many weeks. Once inside the Reich, Allied troops got their first look at Nazi concentration camps as they confronted scenes of horror like the one below.

The Ludendorff Bridge, safely in the hands of Allied troops, stands ready to carry Ike's armies across the Rhine frontier. Ten days after the bridge was taken, the structure, weakened by demolition charges, bombs and shells, collapsed. But by then an auxiliary bridge sturdy enough to take its place had been built.

A horrified Eisenhower, surrounded by death-camp survivors and American officers including General Patton (at Ike's right shoulder), gazes at some of Hitler's victims found at Gotha, first of the Nazi camps that were overrun by Allied troops after their crossing of the Rhine.

"The mission of this Allied force was fulfilled at 0241 local time, May 7, 1945."

Just 11 months and a day after the Normandy landings, the war in Europe comes to an end as the instrument of surrender is signed (left) by representatives of Germany, the Soviet Union and the Western Allies. Top to bottom are Field Marshal Alfred Jodl (Germany), Major General Ivan Suslaparov (U.S.S.R.) and General Walter Bedell Smith (U.S.). Only after the surrender document had been signed did Ike confront Jodl. He sternly asked him if the Germans understood the surrender terms and if they would carry them out. Jodl replied, "Ja." Ike, reminding him that he would be held personally responsible for German compliance with the terms, curtly dismissed him.

Air Chief Marshal Tedder at his side, Ike broadcasts his victory message following the surrender. For the final report he would send to his chiefs, Ike's staff had suggested a number of high-flown introductions. But Ike rejected them for the eloquently concise words —his own—that appear at left.

Their Führer dead by his own hand, their armies smashed, their country in ruins, the Nazi high command face their Allied conquerors across the conference table at Ike's headquarters in Reims. The terms: unconditional surrender. Field Marshal Alfred Jodl, flanked by two of his aides, sits stony-faced at left as he is given the surrender terms by General Bedell Smith (fourth from top at right), who represented Eisenhower.

Returning home for a short visit a month after the end of the war in Europe, Ike raises his arms in his famous victory salute to acknowledge the cheers of a crowd of 27,000 in New York's Polo Grounds; he stayed on to watch the baseball game but saw little of it because so many politicians insisted on meeting him. Everywhere Eisenhower went he was wildly acclaimed; there were ticker-tape parades, decorations, banquets, and a speech before a joint session of Congress

THE ROAD TO THE WHITE HOUSE

6

One thing in particular distinguished Eisenhower from most of the other men who became President of the United States: he did not seek the office; it sought him. In fact, for almost nine years he shunned it altogether, and the more indifferent he was the more insistent became the demands on him to run. As early as 1943, before the invasion of France, he had been suggested as a candidate, a notion he derisively dismissed as "baloney." In 1945 President Truman, visiting Ike in Berlin after Germany's surrender, was reported to have offered him the Presidency in 1948.

A few months later, in the fall of 1945, he returned home, intending to retire, but President Truman assigned him to replace General Marshall as Chief of Staff. For two years Ike remained in this post before realizing a long-cherished ambition to get out of uniform; in May of 1948 he left active duty to become president of Columbia University.

As head of one of the nation's foremost educational institutions, Eisenhower continued to be sought as a Presidential candidate, but still he brushed aside all requests to run. He had been at Columbia about 26 months when President Truman asked him to return to active military duty as Supreme Commander of the North Atlantic Treaty Organization, lending his great prestige to help unify the new coalition of Western nations in a common defense against Communism. Reluctantly, Ike took a leave of absence from Columbia to command NATO in Paris. In this new international spotlight the pressures on him to become a Presidential candidate were greater than ever, and his boosters now included such figures as Governor Thomas E. Dewey of New York, Senator Henry Cabot Lodge of Massachusetts and General Lucius Clay. At first Ike resisted their entreaties, but eventually he let himself be pushed toward his third career in public service.

That spring he made such a strong showing in the New Hampshire and Minnesota primaries that he no longer could deny the mandate to run. In June of 1952 Eisenhower returned home, resigned his Army Commission after 37 years of service, and became a Presidential candidate. In July he defeated Senator Robert Taft of Ohio for the GOP nomination, and on November 4 he won a landslide victory over former Governor Adlai Stevenson of Illinois, sweeping all but nine states.

As president of Columbia, Ike stood behind his desk, hands in pockets, for an informal portrait. His job at the university was complicated by the demands on him to seek the Presidency. Once radio commentator Walter Winchell asked his listeners to write Eisenhower urging him to become a candidate. In the first week, Ike was swamped by some 20,000 letters and cards.

A CHANGE OF CAPS FOR COLUMBIA'S NEW PRESIDENT

Ike and Mamie smile happily while attending ceremonies honoring the general upon his retirement from active duty at Fort Myer, Virginia, in May 1948. He had been in the Army 33 years and was looking forward to civilian life and a new job in education.

In a new kind of uniform, an academic cap and gown, Eisenhower is installed as Columbia's president. Among the spectators were his son John, then an Army captain (second from left); Mamie (foreground), Washington hostess Perle Mesta (next to Ike) and almost hidden behind Mrs. Mesta's hat, General Omar Bradley.

Among the prominent visitors Eisenhower received in his new role was Eleanor Roosevelt, shown chatting with him before she gave a speech at the university in the summer of 1948. In the political atmosphere that was beginning to build around him there was some talk of teaming Ike to run for President with Mrs. Roosevelt as Vice President on the Democratic ticket.

Always a football enthusiast, Ike dropped by a Columbia practice session to meet the team and reminisce about his days as a player on the Academy team at West Point. At the left (in cap) is veteran Coach Lou Little, who had announced his intention of leaving the university for a coaching job at Yale. Ike talked Little into staying on, endearing himself to the alumni.

FROM NATO TO NEW HAMPSHIRE

Eisenhower's reluctance at leaving Columbia to become Supreme Allied Commander for NATO was understandable. It meant giving up a job he liked, tearing up his roots again as he and Mamie had done so many times in the past, and returning to active military duty after he thought he had left it behind forever. But he felt that it was his duty to do as the President asked, and he believed in NATO's objective of providing collective security against the growing Communist menace.

Ike arrived in France to take over his new command at SHAPE (Supreme Headquarters, Allied Powers in Europe) on January 7, 1951. He soon learned that it was as hard to unify allies in peace as in war. The 12 member-countries (later 15) were deeply divided on several basic issues and were often reluctant to make the sacrifices necessary for unity. One of Ike's biggest headaches was France, which feared a rearmed Germany as a member of NATO and also had reservations about the integration of all the striking forces under a single command. In addition, Ike never had enough manpower to fill out the organization's optimistic paper divisions, and at home several congressmen still opposed the idea of contributing ground forces to a peacetime alliance with European countries. Nevertheless, the general visited the member-countries, smoothed over differences between them and raised a unified fighting force that eventually included West German troops.

Along with his problems at NATO, Ike had to contend with an unending parade of politicians who visited his office and his home, just outside of Paris, urging him to seek the Presidency. Representatives of both major parties asked him to run on their ticket. Until then he had never declared his party affiliation, so no one really knew which ticket he was refusing to run on. While keeping his political faith to himself, he continued to insist that he just was not interested in entering politics. The turning point came in early September of 1951 when Senator Lodge, an old friend from World War II days, visited him. Lodge had learned from General Lucius D. Clay that Eisenhower had voted the GOP ticket since he had left the Army in 1948; the Senator represented a powerful group in the United States that wanted Eisenhower to become the party's candidate the following year. Lodge's most telling thrust was that Ike was the only candidate with whom the Republicans could win, and he insisted that Eisenhower permit the use of his name in the coming primaries. At first Ike said no, as usual, but Lodge kept hammering away until finally Ike promised to think it over.

Without formal authorization, Lodge disclosed that Ike was a Republican and entered his name in the New Hampshire primary to be held in March. Ike was immediately besieged by eager newsmen. He confirmed the fact that he was a Republican but refused to go beyond that. A short time later, some 15,000 Eisenhower enthusiasts, including celebrities from the entertainment world such as Fred Waring and Ethel Merman, held an unusual rally in Madison Square Garden at midnight (following a prizefight) on February 8, urging Ike to run. A film was made of the gathering and taken to Paris, where it was shown to Ike and Mamie. The general was deeply touched by this testimonial, and about a week later his old friend General Clay flew to London, where he held a long conference with Ike. Before their meeting was over Ike agreed to take the big step—he would return home as soon as he could wind up his NATO duties, and, if the Republican convention nominated him, he would campaign actively for the Presidency.

Eisenhower was still in Europe with NATO when the New Hampshire primary was held on March 11, a cold, blustery day that did little to encourage voters to go to the polls, but he bested his major rival, Senator Robert A. Taft, by some 10,000 votes. A week later, his great popularity was demonstrated even more forcefully in the Minnesota primary; although his name was not on the ballot and he had never campaigned in any way, he received a total of more than 100,000 write-in votes.

Politics were now disrupting Ike's life to such an extent that he realized he could not continue in his NATO assignment and do justice to the job. Nor could he deny the mandate that had been thrust upon him. At his request, he was relieved from his NATO command duties and returned home. If nominated, he said, he was ready to accept the Republican Party's Presidential candidacy.

Standing on the Acropolis, Ike and fellow officers chat with a Parthenon guide while Eisenhower was in Athens visiting officers of the Greek force that had recently joined NATO. The photograph was taken just a few days before the New Hampshire primary.

ONE OLD SOLDIER VIEWS ANOTHER

As Eisenhower rose to equal and even greater prominence than his old boss, Douglas MacArthur, their differences were occasionally played upon by the press. When asked his opinion, Mac was once reported to have described Ike as "the best clerk who ever served under me." For his part, Ike was pleased to have "studied dramatics" under MacArthur. While Eisenhower was still with NATO, MacArthur was relieved of his command in Korea for opposing the Truman administration's policy by advocating an attack on Red China. In the public furor that followed, MacArthur returned home and addressed a joint session of Congress in an emotional speech, romanticizing his role in the dispute and bidding a melodramatic farewell *(below)*, amid rumors that he, too, might run for President. Ike's reaction to the firing was, characteristically, a classic expression *(right)*, and his own terse summation of the facts of military life *(bottom)*.

"... And like the old soldier of that ballad, I now close my military career and just fade away, an old soldier who tried to do his duty as God gave him the light to see that duty. Goodbye."

"When you put on a uniform, there are certain inhibitions you accept."

While Eisenhower refused all pleas to run for the Presidency, the pressure on him continued relentlessly as buttons, playing cards, bracelets and kerchiefs proclaimed the famous motto "I like Ike." A syndicated comic strip by Ding (J. N. Darling) poked fun at his supporters who refused to take no for an answer.

At the right Ike gives an eloquent, wordless reply to the inevitable question of whether he intended to seek the Presidency. This celebrated photograph was taken in Copenhagen in January 1951, a few weeks after he had assumed command of NATO.

A VICTORIOUS CONVENTION

Once Ike made his decision to run, there was still no guarantee that he would get the nomination. Despite the general's tremendous popularity, Senator Taft's vigorous campaigning had gained him a substantial lead in pledged delegate votes. As the party began gathering in Chicago to hold its convention on July 7, Taft had a total of about 500 delegate votes, and Eisenhower had about the same number. It appeared that the delegates of Minnesota and California held the balance of power—along with 68 votes from the bitterly contested delegations from Texas, Georgia and Louisiana.

The convention got underway with General MacArthur delivering the keynote speech. An abortive effort was made by some of his supporters to generate enthusiasm for his nomination. But it was overshadowed by the fight for the crucial contested delegates so desperately needed by Taft and Ike for their own chances of nomination. In the end, Eisenhower's supporters won out, and managed to get him nominated on the first ballot; Minnesota's 19 votes, switched to Ike from Harold Stassen, were the final cap to victory. In the aftermath of the balloting, it seemed that all Eisenhower's powers of conciliation would be needed to re-unify the party and persuade the embittered followers of Taft to support him in the coming campaign.

NEW HAMPSHIRE (ballot vote)		MINNESOTA (write-in vote)	
Eisenhower	46,661	Eisenhower	108,692
Taft	35,838	Taft	24,093

As Minnesota switched its votes to Eisenhower, giving him the nomination, the convention erupted into a wild demonstration, with delegates parading and the organ thundering. Preconvention pictures of the two rivals are shown at the left, reflecting the moods they must have felt after the New Hampshire and Minnesota primaries, which forecast the outcome of the convention. (Listed between the pictures are the primary results.)

FOR U.S.
Mr. AMERICA
likes
IKE
FOR
IKE

Eisenhower and Richard Nixon (above), GOP Vice Presidential candidate in 1952, meet for the first time following charges of fiscal improprieties. Nixon, the press reported, financed some political expenses with an $18,000 fund contributed by California businessmen. Spurred by an Eisenhower statement that Nixon must come out of the affair as "clean as a hound's tooth," the Vice Presidential candidate cleared himself in the famous "Checkers" TV speech, turning what looked like disaster into a campaign triumph.

At campaign's end, Ike and Mamie (right) wave to a cheering, singing crowd at the Hotel Commodore in New York after the voters' decision was plain—Eisenhower rolled up a 6.6-million-vote plurality over Adlai Stevenson, shown below conceding defeat.

THE BUSY PURSUIT OF A MIDDLE COURSE

7

To the Presidency, Eisenhower brought a deeply "civilian" philosophy that was at sharp variance with the stereotype of the soldier-politician whose thinking is colored in only two ideological shades: black and white. Much of Ike's success as an Allied commander had depended on his ability to sense the diverse needs and feelings of others and forge them into a consensus. In the White House—an office that, as Ike well knew, had to be responsive to a clamor of divergent public interests—he tried to project the experience he had gained as a commander onto the wider stage of Presidential policy. His watchwords were pragmatism, accommodation, the middle course. A Republican whose ideas had been formed long before the Roosevelt era, he nevertheless recognized the New Deal as a fact of life; he never saw his own Republicanism as an ideological mandate to erase the marks left by five Democratic administrations. Above all, in a world of violently antagonistic ideologies, he saw the road to peace as a middle way that avoided both provocation of and capitulation to the adversary.

In pursuit of peace, Ike had kept his campaign promise to go to Korea even before his inauguration, and six months after assuming office his administration ended the three-year war that had cost more than two million killed, wounded and missing. Korea, half Communist and half non-Communist, reverted to its prewar status—a compromise that Ike regarded as "an acceptable solution." Throughout his administration, Eisenhower was bedeviled not only with the threat of Communism abroad, but also by the dark shadow it cast at home. Postwar revelations that American citizens had sold or given military secrets to the Soviets led to a series of trials, government firings and security hearings—and an atmosphere of "Red scare" and witch-hunt that was made to order for a skillful, ruthless demagogue. In Joseph McCarthy, ju-

Framed by a bouquet of roses, Eisenhower sits behind the massive desk in the White House on his first day in office. Most of the day was spent shaking hands, receiving congratulations and discussing official appointments. In the afternoon the new White House staff was sworn in and the President said to them, "Gentlemen, I want the White House to be an example to the nation."

nior Republican Senator from Wisconsin, the hour found its man: brandishing "lists" of subversives, claiming to know the names of hundreds of card-carrying Communists in government jobs, McCarthy hurled reckless charges of treason. The reputations of many innocent people were sullied or destroyed forever, and the country suffered a nightmare of doubt and suspicion.

Ike chose to deal with McCarthy by ignoring him, telling his intimates that he would not lower the prestige of his office by getting down in the gutter with the Wisconsin Senator. For this aloof stand he was loudly condemned: McCarthyites accused him of being soft on Communism; the Senator's foes charged Ike with tolerating demagoguery. Finally, McCarthy went too far and brought about his own downfall. The beginning of the end came when he took on the U.S. Army, insisting that he had the right to question members of its loyalty-review board and examine individual security files. The Army, firmly backed by Eisenhower, refused these demands and retaliated by accusing McCarthy of trying to get preferential treatment for one of his former aides, a young man who had been drafted. The dispute led to the famous Army-McCarthy hearings, which resulted in McCarthy's censure by the Senate and his consequent loss of power—an outcome that Ike felt vindicated his handling of the situation.

With the decline of McCarthyism, there were also hopeful signs of a lessening of tension in the Cold War—particularly in the convening of the first postwar "summit conference," attended by Ike and Soviet Chairman Nikita Khrushchev in Geneva in the summer of 1955. There Eisenhower introduced his "Open Skies" plan, calling on East and West to permit aerial inspection of their defenses in order to reduce the chances for a surprise attack by either side. Ultimately the Russians turned the plan down, insisting it was merely a screen for espionage, but Ike felt that the meeting had at least opened the way for more cordial relations—including various cultural and trade exchanges.

Only a few weeks after the summit meeting, in late September, Eisenhower's career came to an abrupt, if temporary, halt. The country was shocked by news that the President had suffered a heart attack in Denver, where he had gone on a work-play vacation. In the ensuing days a flood of medical bulletins poured out as Eisenhower, remembering public criticism of the secrecy shrouding the illnesses of Presidents Wilson and Franklin Roosevelt, insisted that the people should be told the full truth about his health and his ability to continue in office. Only when convinced that he would make a full recovery did he announce—on February 29—that he would seek a second term.

With his return to health, Eisenhower resumed a full schedule of official duties. During the weeks between the Republican convention—where Ike was renominated unanimously on the first ballot—and the national elections that gave Eisenhower his second landslide victory, two foreign crises erupted. They were to put Eisenhower's powers of calmness and resolution to the fullest test. When the Hungarians rebelled against their Soviet masters the temptation to go to their aid was strong—and was only put to rest by the onslaught of Soviet military power that snuffed out the revolt.

When the British and French—Ike's old allies—backed an Israeli attack on Egypt, the temptation to support them was perhaps greater. Not only was there the call of international friendship, but Egypt's President Gamal Abdel Nasser was, in the opinion of Eisenhower, a disruptive, cynical dictator whose continued leadership threatened the very possibility of peace in the Middle East. But the attackers had violated international agreements—and given the Soviets grounds for a stand with Nasser. The risks of a major East-West confrontation—and World War III—were too great: the Soviets threatened to intervene on the side of Egypt if the British and French did not withdraw. Eisenhower had little choice: reluctantly but firmly, he had to lean on his friends in Paris and London to pull their troops out of the Middle East.

At Eisenhower's first meeting with fellow heads-of-government (in Bermuda, December 1956) he takes the arm of the aging Prime Minister Churchill (who was then 82) as they approach steps on their way to sit for photographs. France's Premier Joseph Laniel stands with his back to the camera.

Upon his return from Bermuda on December 8, Eisenhower, introducing his "Atoms for Peace" plan, addresses the U.N. General Assembly (above). The proposal called on the nuclear nations to pool their fissionable materials and use them to develop nuclear energy for peaceful purposes.

Joseph Welch, the peppery lawyer hired by the Army to defend it against Senator Joseph McCarthy's charges that it harbored Communists, makes a point during the 1954 hearings. With his caustic wit and unbudgeable honesty, Welch was able to make McCarthy hold his tongue (right)—turning aside McCarthy's techniques of bluster and innuendo that had worked so well against hapless targets in the past. In the end, a tearful McCarthy (below) listened to the Senate clerk read his colleagues' vote of censure—and was heard no more.

"Senator McCarthy died an untimely and sad—even pathetic—death in 1957, but as a political force he was finished at the end of 1954."—Eisenhower ("Mandate for Change")

THE DOWNFALL OF A DEMAGOGUE

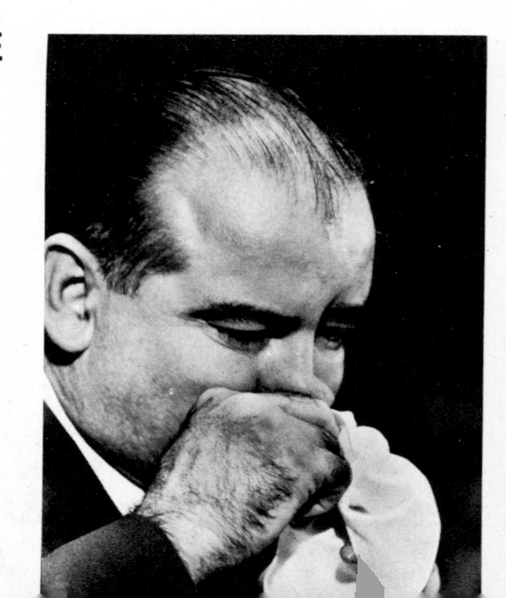

SUNDAY NEWS

NEW YORK'S PICTURE NEWSPAPER®

Vol. 35. No. 22 Copr. 1955 News Syndicate Co. Inc. New York 17, N.Y., Sunday, September 25, 1955★ 4 Sections | MAIN SECTION TWO MAGAZINE COMICS

IKE SUFFERS HEART ATTACK

—Story on Page 3

(Associated Press foto)

Day before he was stricken with heart attack, smiling President arrived in Denver. This was before he played 27 holes of golf. ***—Story p. 3***

In a 10-week summary of daily stock averages published in "The New York Times," arrows bracket the plunge taken by the stock market on the Monday following Ike's attack. The market took the sharpest dive since the Crash—Black Monday, October 29, 1929.

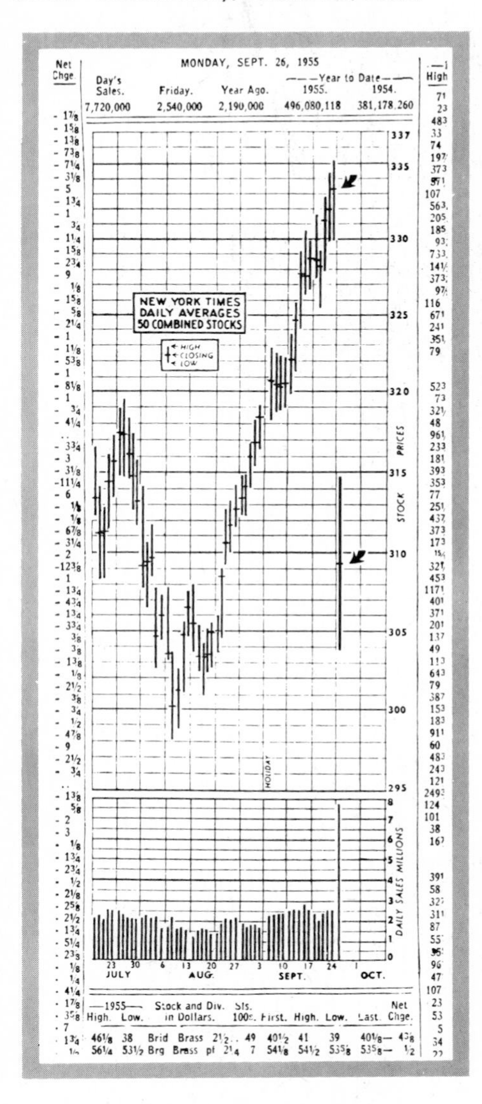

The suddenness of Ike's coronary thrombosis is dramatized in the headlines at left—printed in the New York "Daily News" above a photograph of an apparently healthy President taken the day before the attack. In the famous photograph at right, Ike—on the road to recovery—goes for a wheel-chair ride, his pajamas embroidered with an upbeat message the cameras could not fail to get.

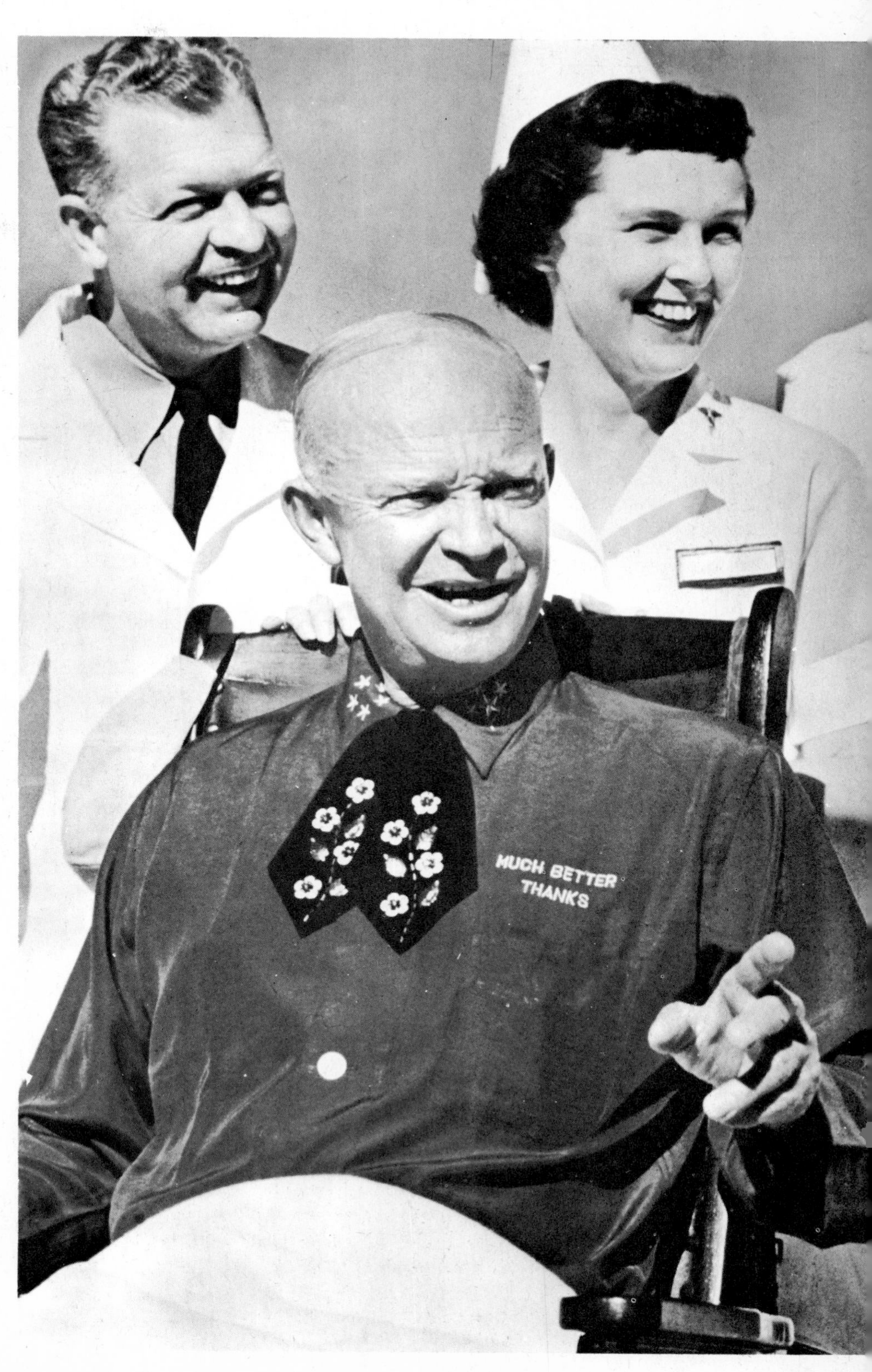

David Eisenhower, age 5, bows in a courtly greeting (left) that obviously delights his grandfather the President. The meeting took place at the golf course at Augusta, Georgia, where the Eisenhowers, on a first-term golfing holiday, had a cottage. David, who was visiting, wandered away and suddenly popped up on the course to shake hands with his grandfather.

Carrying his granddaughter, Barbara Anne (foreground), the President mixes with a huge crowd at the Easter egg-rolling festivities on the White House lawn; just to his left, a Presidential aide leads David by the hand. Soon after he took office, Ike revived the egg-rolling tradition, which began during the Grant administration (1873-1877) but later lapsed.

A TANDEM OF CRISES

Rioters in Budapest burn a portrait of Stalin during the Hungarian uprising of 1956. The revolt lasted 13 days before it was crushed by overwhelming Soviet military power; almost 50,000 Hungarians were killed, and 200,000 fled the country. Under an emergency immigration program initiated by Ike, the U.S. admitted 40,000 of the refugees.

The tense expressions on the faces of President Eisenhower and Secretary of State Dulles convey the grimness of the international situation as they emerge from a conference on the Middle East on October 30—the day after Israel launched its attack on Egypt through the Sinai Desert.

British troops stand guard on the Suez Canal while a ship burns in the distance—the aftermath of the British bombing of Port Said. Under terms of a U.N. cease-fire resolution introduced by the United States, the fighting ended on November 7, the day after Ike was re-elected for a second term.

Ike beams at the wild victory demonstration at the GOP National Convention on August 23, 1956. He was renominated unanimously on the first ballot by the 1,323 delegates. Beside him, facing away from the camera, are Mamie and Vice President Nixon; behind them are Major and Mrs. John Eisenhower.

Ike stands with arms upraised, beside the Nixons, as he is acclaimed in Washington's Sheraton Park Hotel on election night. The scoreboard at right indicates the size of his victory: he had been too busy to campaign much, but he won the biggest popular vote up to that time—35,590,472 to Stevenson's 26,022,752.

EISENHOWER
ALA.
149,329
ARIZ.
90,338
51,878
ARK.
35123
48991
CALIF.
475,226
389,007
COLO.
102,871
CONN.
710,059
406,561
DEL
92,328
FLA
512,308
GA
IDAHO

POLITICS IN THE SPACE AGE

8

Considering "this shaken earth" in his second inaugural address, Dwight Eisenhower referred to the harsh winds of change that were blowing across the troubled face of the globe. People both abroad and at home were clamoring, in Eisenhower's words "almost in desperation" for freedom from ancient oppression and material want; radical breakthroughs in technology held out both promises and threats to their aspirations.

The first domestic evidence of this stormy change that Eisenhower had to confront in his second term grew out of the landmark decision on school desegregation handed down by the U.S. Supreme Court in 1954. In September 1957, nine Negro children tried to enroll at the all-white Central High School in Little Rock, Arkansas. Their way was blocked by National Guard troops sent to the school by Arkansas Governor Orval Faubus. Complying with a federal court order, Faubus eventually removed the Guardsmen, the children again tried to enter, and the school was surrounded by an ugly mob that the Little Rock police could not—or would not—control. The children had to be removed from school for their own safety. Such disregard of a federal court order forced Eisenhower to intervene. As a last resort, and believing that only anarchy and contempt for the Constitution could result from a failure to act, he sent Regular Army paratroopers to Little Rock to enforce the law of the land. The desegregation orders—backed up by federal bayonets—were obeyed, but the President felt the lash of criticism as he never had before. Georgia's Senator Richard Russell compared the dis-

Following a tradition begun under Woodrow Wilson, President Eisenhower conducts a White House press conference (center panel); the pictures around the edge show the range of his expressions, from amusement to deep thoughtfulness, as he reacts to newsmen.

FACING THE HARSH WINDS OF CHANGE

patch of U.S. troops to the Nazis' use of Storm Troopers; Northern liberals complained that Eisenhower had acted too late in upholding the orders of the court.

The wounds of Little Rock were still festering when another hurricane of change struck the nation with the news that a Russian space satellite, called "Sputnik," had been blasted into orbit. Overnight, Sputnik inaugurated the space age—and shattered America's complacent assumption of its scientific and technological superiority and its confidence in its national security. To many, the Soviet space feat revealed a disturbing fact: the Russians had a rocket booster that had easily thrust a heavy payload into space. Did it mean, people asked, that with equal ease similar boosters could hurl intercontinental ballistic missiles at the U.S., which then had no ICBM capability? The President quickly reassured the nation that its defenses were adequate; he said that he, personally, felt no apprehension. His reputation as a military man was so great, his confidence so convincing, that the tide of fear receded.

But Sputnik, the frightening creature of a foreign adversary, had a salutary effect at home. Many Americans, wondering whether Sputnik meant that the Russians were more competent scientifically than the U.S., raised questions about American scientific education that reverberated through the nation's school systems. The resulting ferment—which the Russians had inadvertently stirred up—pumped new money and fresh thinking into the nation's schools. It culminated in a revolution of teaching (and learning) standards that still continues.

About six weeks after Sputnik had jolted the nation, Eisenhower suffered his third major illness in as many years—the "stroke" that affected his speech and memory and once more cast doubt on his ability to continue in the Presidency. But again he made an astonishing, gallant and rapid recovery; by December 17 he was able to attend an important NATO meeting in Paris where he read a paper. Only later he revealed that he had been testing himself and had he not been able to perform to his satisfaction he would have resigned.

The winds of change in Dwight Eisenhower's second term struck hard at his White House family. He lost two men he depended on above all others. Death took his brilliant, trusted Secretary of State, John Foster Dulles. And his Presidential Assistant and chief of staff, Sherman Adams, resigned under a cloud of scandal.

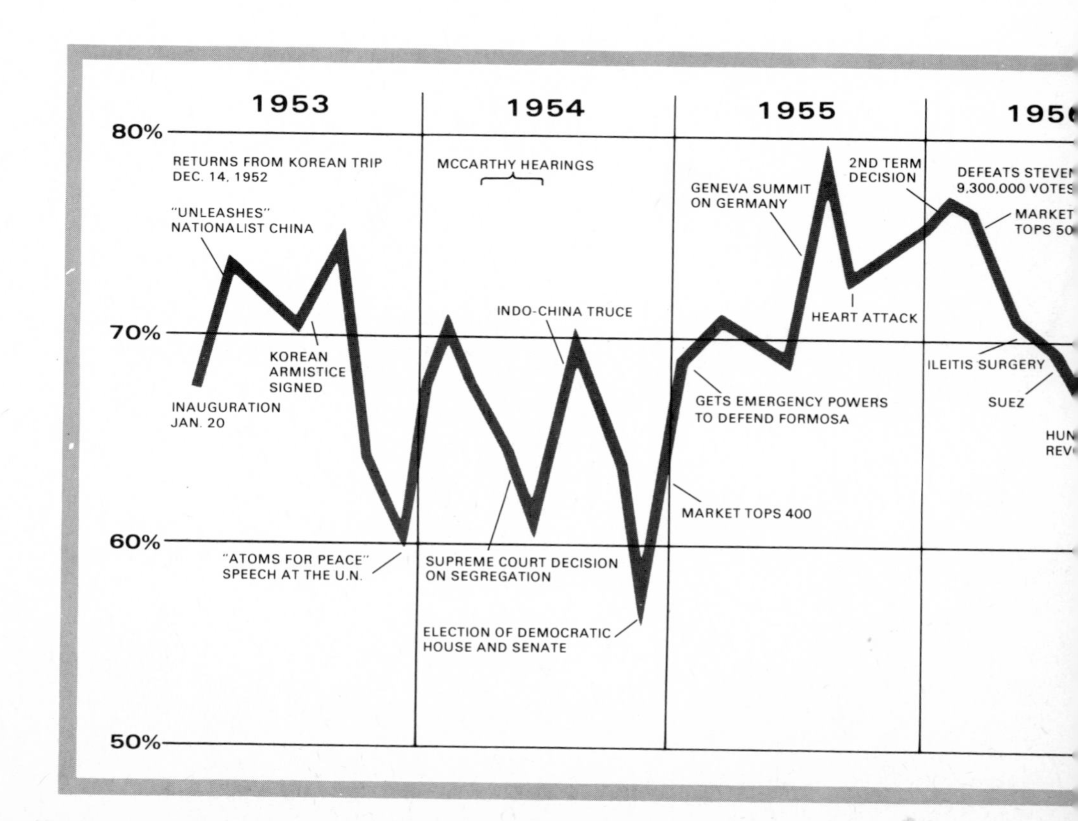

To Eisenhower, Adams—a former Governor of New Hampshire—was the apotheosis of New England rectitude. Simple in his tastes, frugal in his habits, Adams was the last person Ike would have suspected of improperly accepting gifts from someone for whom he might have been expected to do a favor in return. Yet that is precisely what Adams was accused by the press of having done. The stories said that Bernard Goldfine, a New England textile manufacturer and businessman whom Adams had known for more than a decade, had given Adams a vicuña coat worth $500 and an Oriental rug. Adams was also charged with having stayed in a Boston hotel at Goldfine's expense. In congressional hearings at which he volunteered to testify, Adams admitted accepting the gifts, but denied having made any deals with federal regulatory agencies for Goldfine. Eisenhower accepted Adams's version of the affair and loyally kept him in his post. Only when Republican party leaders insisted that keeping Adams in the government would hand the Democrats too much campaign ammunition in the 1958 congressional elections was Ike reluctantly forced to accept his resignation.

Dulles fell ill with cancer in 1958, but until the Secretary of State became so weak that he could no longer receive visitors, Eisenhower continued to consult him. But even before Dulles' death in May 1959, the President had to change his ways of conducting foreign policy. The answer—a painful one after the years of reliance on Dulles—was personal diplomacy *(pages 116-117)*.

As Ike's second term drew to a close, his personal approaches to the problems of the world through its people were at first accompanied by a surge of his popularity with the people at home *(see chart below)*. It was only when the Cold War seemed, in mid-1960, to be on the boil again that his popularity fell off.

Indeed, it was one of the President's great disappointments that as his term drew to an end East and West were no closer than they were at his inauguration. Another disappointment was Vice President Richard Nixon's failure to win the Presidency in 1960; not even Ike's support was enough to swing the election, and on November 8, 1960, Senator John F. Kennedy was elected by a narrow margin. On January 20, 1961, Eisenhower turned the government over to his young successor, and shortly thereafter he left for his home at Gettysburg—the first he could call his own since leaving Abilene in 1911.

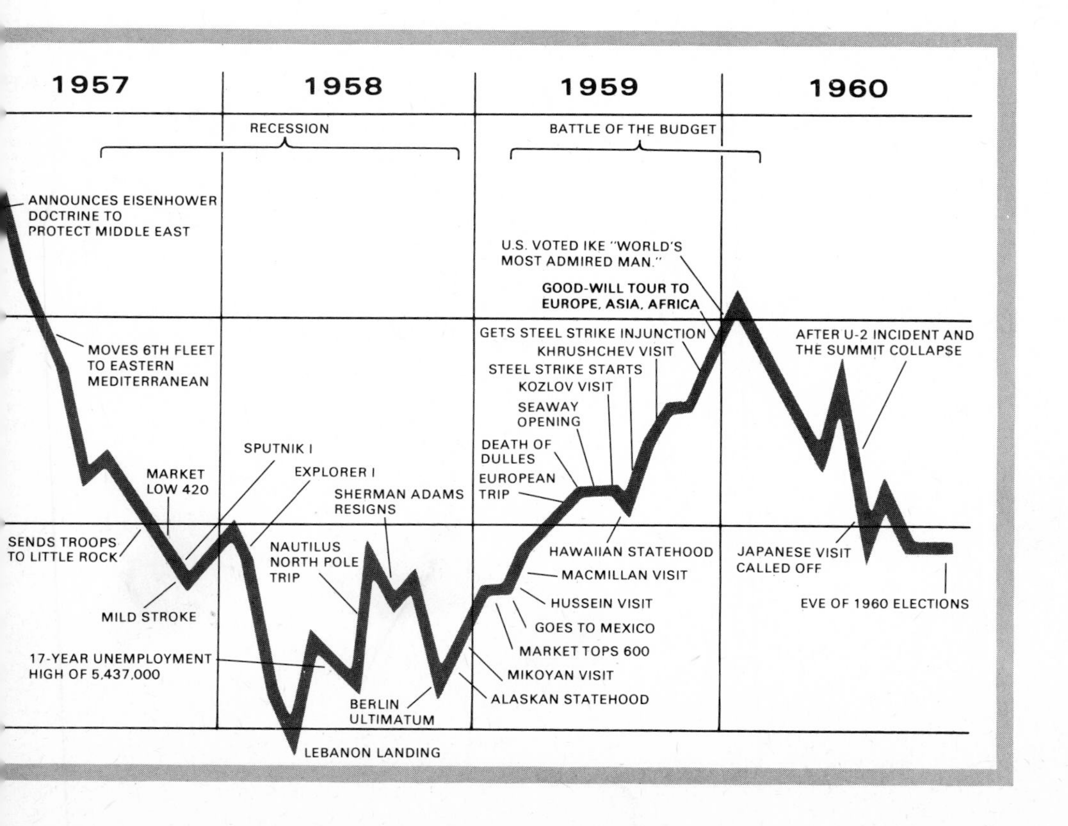

LITTLE ROCK AND THE LAW OF THE LAND

Soldiers of the 101st Airborne Division, the same unit Ike saw off to France the evening before D-Day in World War II, stand guard as Negro students go home from newly desegregated Central High School in Little Rock. The children were taken to and from school in cars to protect them from the mob.

Governor Orval Faubus of Arkansas appears on television in Little Rock to accuse the federal troops sent there by Eisenhower of using violence on white students. The picture he holds purports to show the soldiers roughing up students—part of a campaign that helped him gain his fourth term as governor.

A youth who had been protesting integration —and the presence of the troops in Little Rock —is led away from the scene of disturbance by bayonet-armed paratroopers. The federal soldiers stood guard until school ended for the year. In the fall of 1958, Negro students were admitted for the first time without trouble.

IN A STIR OF SCANDAL, A BITTER TEST OF LOYALTY

An impassioned Eisenhower defends Sherman Adams during a press conference in June 1958, shortly after Adams voluntarily testified before a congressional committee.

"As a result of this entire incident, all of us should have been made aware of one truth. That is, that a gift is not necessarily a bribe. . . ."

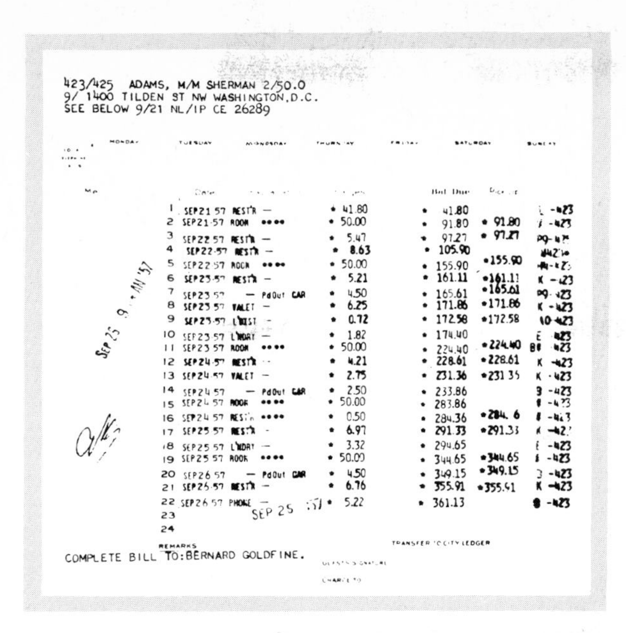

423/425 ADAMS, M/M SHERMAN 2/50.0
9/ 1400 TILDEN ST NW WASHINGTON, D.C.
SEE BELOW 9/21 NL/IP CE 26289

	Date				Bal Due		
1	SEP21 57	RESTR —		• 41.80	• 41.80		-423
2	SEP21 57	ROOM ••••		• 50.00	• 91.80	• 91.80	-423
3	SEP22 57	RESTR —		• 5.47	• 97.27	• 97.27	PQ-423
4	SEP22 57	RESTR —		• 8.63	• 105.90		[illegible]
5	SEP22 57	ROOM ••••		• 50.00	• 155.90	•155.90	[illegible]
6	SEP23 57	RESTR —		• 5.21	• 161.11	•161.11	K -423
7	SEP23 57	—	PdOut CAR	• 4.50	• 165.61	•165.61	PQ-423
8	SEP23 57	VALET —		• 6.25	• 171.86	•171.86	K -423
9	SEP23 57	LDIST —		• 0.72	• 172.58	•172.58	10-423
10	SEP23 57	LNDRY —		• 1.82	• 174.40		E 423
11	SEP23 57	ROOM ••••		• 50.00	• 224.40	•224.40	B 423
12	SEP24 57	RESTR —		• 4.21	• 228.61	•228.61	K -423
13	SEP24 57	VALET —		• 2.75	• 231.36	•231.35	K -423
14	SEP24 57	—	PdOut CAR	• 2.50	• 233.86		3 -423
15	SEP24 57	ROOM ••••		• 50.00	• 283.86		-423
16	SEP24 57	RESTR ••••		• 0.50	• 284.36	•284.6	-423
17	SEP25 57	RESTR —		• 6.97	• 291.33	•291.33	K -423
18	SEP25 57	LNDRY —		• 3.32	• 294.65		E -423
19	SEP25 57	ROOM ••••		• 50.00	• 344.65	•344.65	-423
20	SEP26 57	—	PdOut CAR	• 4.50	• 349.15	•349.15	3 -423
21	SEP26 57	RESTR —		• 6.76	• 355.91	•355.91	K -423
22	SEP26 57	PHONE —		• 5.22	• 361.13		-423
23							
24							

SEP 25 9 AM '57

SEP 25 '57

REMARKS
COMPLETE BILL TO: BERNARD GOLDFINE.

TRANSFER TO CITY LEDGER

Backing charges that Presidential Assistant Sherman Adams had accepted gifts, the press published this copy of an itemized bill covering his stay in the Sheraton-Plaza Hotel in Boston from September 21-26, 1957. A note shows that the bill, which came to $361.13, was to be paid by Bernard Goldfine.

Adams announces his resignation from his White House job in a televised speech on September 22, 1958. He charged that he had been the victim of a "campaign of vilification" and was quitting only out of "consideration to the effect of my continuing presence on the public scene."

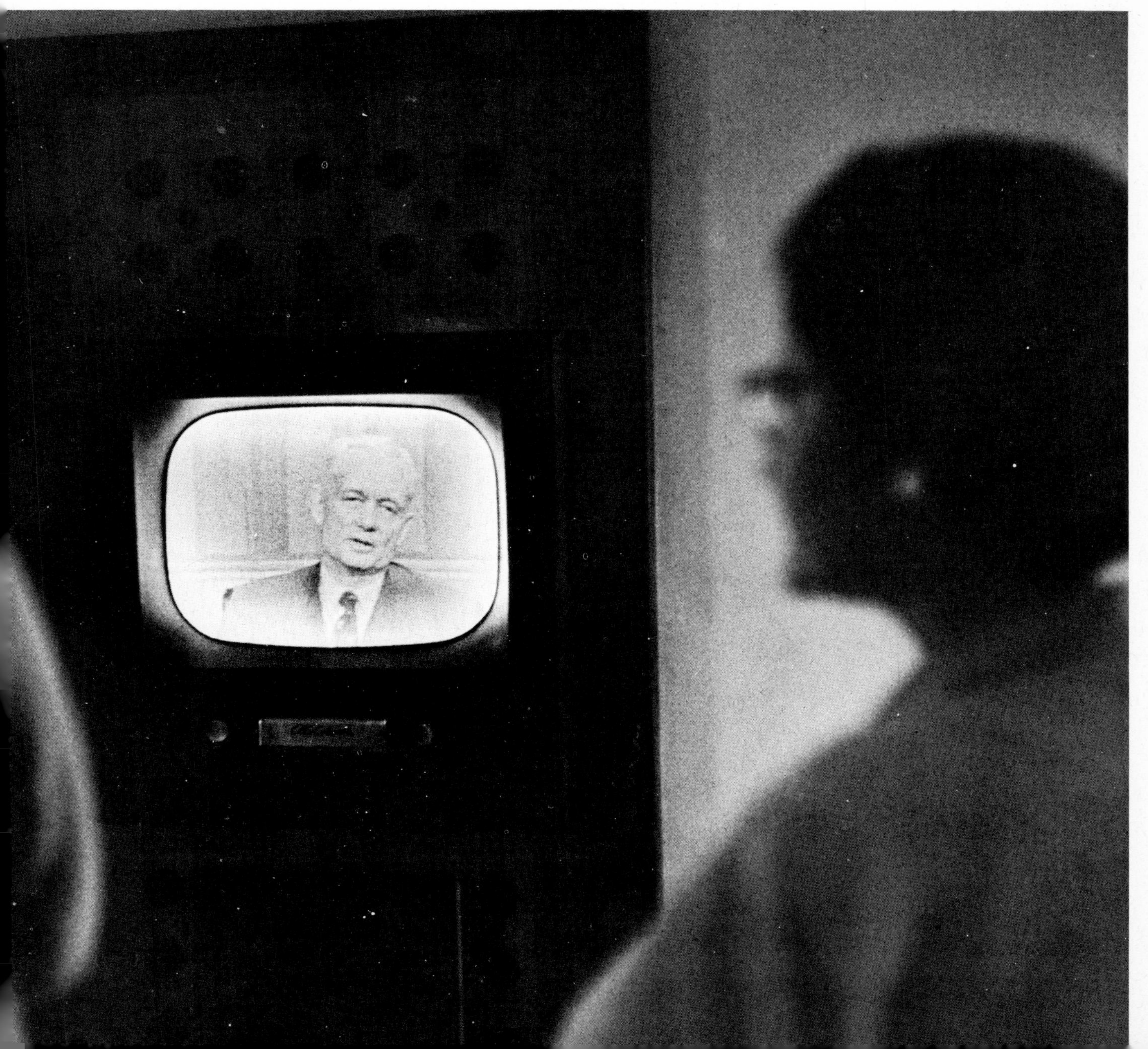

On a visit by Winston Churchill to the U.S. in the spring of 1959, Ike accompanies him to Walter Reed Hospital to pay a call on John Foster Dulles, who was soon to die of cancer. For the three old friends, the meeting, last of its kind, was particularly poignant.

SEEKING TO COOL OFF THE COLD WAR

By 1958, crises in foreign affairs had, in Eisenhower's words, become "normalcy." The specter of trouble in the Middle East loomed in May when Communist political activity in Syria and Iraq seemed likely to spill into tiny Lebanon. At the request of Lebanese President Camille Chamoun, Eisenhower sent U.S. troops to make sure that the government would not be overthrown. Cuba —only 90 miles from the U.S. mainland—became a hostile Communist satellite. Berlin, the East-West pressure point that had always had the most potential for Cold War trouble, felt the heavy Russian thumb when Soviet Premier Khrushchev threatened to sign a separate "peace treaty" with Communist East Germany and abrogate the Four-Power Agreements that gave the Allies access to the beleaguered city.

Eisenhower's answer to the Kremlin's truculence after the death of Dulles in 1959 was personal diplomacy.

The President set himself a supreme challenge, telling legislative leaders that he wanted to make "one great personal effort, before leaving office, to soften up the Soviet leader even a little bit." He invited Khrushchev to visit the United States in the fall of 1959; Ike planned to go to Russia the following year. Ike looked forward to the visits with only a little hope of real results; his misgivings increased following the breakdown of plans for a meeting of U.S., British, French and Soviet heads of government. On his arrival in America, the stout Russian Premier galloped about the country, trailed by panting newsmen, nervous security officers and State Department officials; in his wake he left a backwash of jokes, threats, Russian proverbs and propaganda. A highly publicized meeting with Ike at Camp David confirmed Eisenhower's fears and produced little in the way of results, although Khrushchev did withdraw his threat to sign a peace treaty with East Germany.

With his time in the Presidency drawing to a close, forbidden by law to seek a third term, Ike undertook one of the great adventures in his administration—a personal peace offensive throughout the world "to assure all the people I could reach of the sincerity of our search for peace and our desire to be helpful."

Ike's first journey, in December of 1959, covered 11 countries in the Mediterranean area and Indian subcontinent. Everywhere he was accorded an enthusiastic welcome by the people and their leaders. In India he addressed a joint session of Parliament, and at the finish the members tapped on their desks with open palms. The President was a little startled until assured that this demonstration was the Indian equivalent of bringing down the house.

The trip proved so successful that in February he made a similar swing throughout Latin America, where there had been much hostile feeling against the United States. But in Sao Paulo, Brazil, thousands stood under dripping umbrellas, throwing soaked confetti and shouting, "Viva Eeke!" In Rio he was delighted by the spectacle of jammed streets and one band after another playing, "God Bless America." Less enchanting were other signs that proclaimed, "We like Ike; we like Fidel too."

In May the President went to Paris to attend another summit meeting, but just before it was slated to start, an American U-2—a high-altitude reconnaissance plane —was shot down over the U.S.S.R. In an explosive outburst, Khrushchev demanded that Eisenhower denounce the U-2 reconnaissance flights and promise they would be discontinued. He insisted that Eisenhower "pass severe judgment" on those responsible. Ike rejected such hypocrisy: the summit collapsed before it started; the trip he was supposed to take to Russia that summer was also cancelled. Eisenhower then decided to carry his campaign to the Far East. It was not an unqualified success; he went to the Philippines, Korea and Formosa, but a scheduled visit to Tokyo had to be called off after Communist-inspired riots broke out protesting his visit.

Upon the President's return home, he ran into an unexpected barrage of criticism. Because of what had transpired in Japan, the press had suddenly soured on Eisenhower's visits to other lands. Eisenhower, wounded by these unexpected barbs, defended his trips as having strengthened the bonds of friendship between nations. In a nationwide broadcast he observed that due to the short time he would remain in office he would not take any more trips, and for the rest of his administration he confined himself to his office in the White House.

A dove—shown carrying a United States flag—was one of scores released by the Greeks to symbolize the peaceful nature of Eisenhower's mission when he visited Athens.

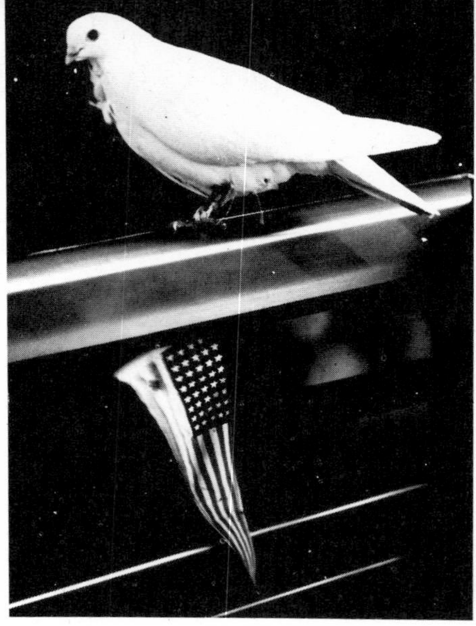

Cheering, massed throngs listen to Eisenhower as he speaks in Karachi, the capital of Pakistan, where he was welcomed by cries of "Take back our love, Ike."

Eisenhower performs his last official act in office, escorting his successor from the White House to the inaugural ceremony on January 20, 1961 (left). In the panel below, Ike shakes hands with the new President after the ceremony. (Distinguished guests are identified below the picture.) Ike, at 70, was the oldest man ever to retire from the Presidency, while Kennedy, at 43, was the youngest elected to the nation's highest office.

HUGO BLACK
RICHARD CARDINAL CUSHING
LYNDON BAINES JOHNSON
RICHARD M. NIXON
THOMAS C. CLARK
ARCHBISHOP IAKOVOS
JOHN SPARKMAN
MARIAN ANDERSON
JOHN W. McCORMACK
HARRY S. TRUMAN
BESS TRUMAN
SAMUEL T. RAYBURN

Leaving the Presidency after eight years, Ike walks alone among shadows cast by the winter sunshine on the White House portico (left). Minutes later the former President and Mrs. Eisenhower left for Gettysburg and a long-awaited retirement, over roads touched with snow that fell on the eve of Kennedy's inaugural; at right, a band of supporters gathers on the road to send him on his way.

A LIFE AT HIS OWN PACE

Even after leaving the Presidency, Eisenhower never really retired in the full sense of the word. His influence was still too great, his own interests too active and widespread not to require an outlet. But now he could work at his own pace; no longer was he under the terrible pressure of responsibility borne by a five-star general or a President of the United States—and he could get in a round of golf when he felt like it without criticism from the opposition or sniping from the press.

Through his great prestige, Eisenhower continued to have a powerful, if subtle, voice in political affairs. Leaders of his own party sought his advice and support. He also played a behind-the-scenes role in helping select Republican candidates for top offices, sometimes negatively by withholding his support. He was kept informed about international affairs by the incumbent Democratic administrations.

But it was the 190-acre farm at Gettysburg that occupied most of his time and gave him the greatest pleasure; there he and Mamie lived a quiet, almost idyllic life as he worked to restore the fertility of the land and supervised the care of his herd of Angus cattle and the half-dozen horses he kept for his grandchildren.

Each day Eisenhower went to a small office in the former residence of the President of Gettysburg College; there he worked from 7:30 a.m. to 4 p.m., dictating his memoirs and answering a flood of letters, which sometimes brought bizarre requests for gifts and mementos. At night he would read or watch television with Mrs. Eisenhower. Visitors to the farm were unanimous in saying that the former President was relaxed and happy in the twilight of his life, and not even the specter of recurring illness that hung over him ever seemed to dampen his ardor for life or to quench the gallant spirit that enabled him to live it so fully.

Pleased as punch after sinking a birdie putt in a match at Ardmore, Pennsylvania, in the spring of 1964, Ike walks jauntily off the green. His partner in the game was then three-time Masters champion Arnold Palmer (right), who seems to share the spectators' delight in watching the former President play.

Campaigning for Republican candidates in the 1962 congressional elections, Eisenhower, shown here at a rally in Hartford, Connecticut, attacked the Kennedy administration's "unconscionable grab of power" and its "sophisticated nonsense."

GHS
IKE

Former President Eisenhower, holding his hat behind him, walks along a path at Camp David with President Kennedy as they earnestly discuss the Bay of Pigs crisis in 1961. Ike was kept informed about foreign affairs and his successors often sought his advice.

During a 1962 visit to Culzean Castle in Ayrshire, Scotland, Ike and Mamie are warmly greeted by the vicar and local congregation of a nearby church where they attended services. Eisenhower had been given a life-time tenancy in the castle after World War II by the British government; in retirement, he sometimes used it as a base for Scottish golfing holidays.

Standing in front of a panoply of pistols in Culzean Castle's armory, Ike beams at his audience while making a speech over the British Broadcasting System in 1962.

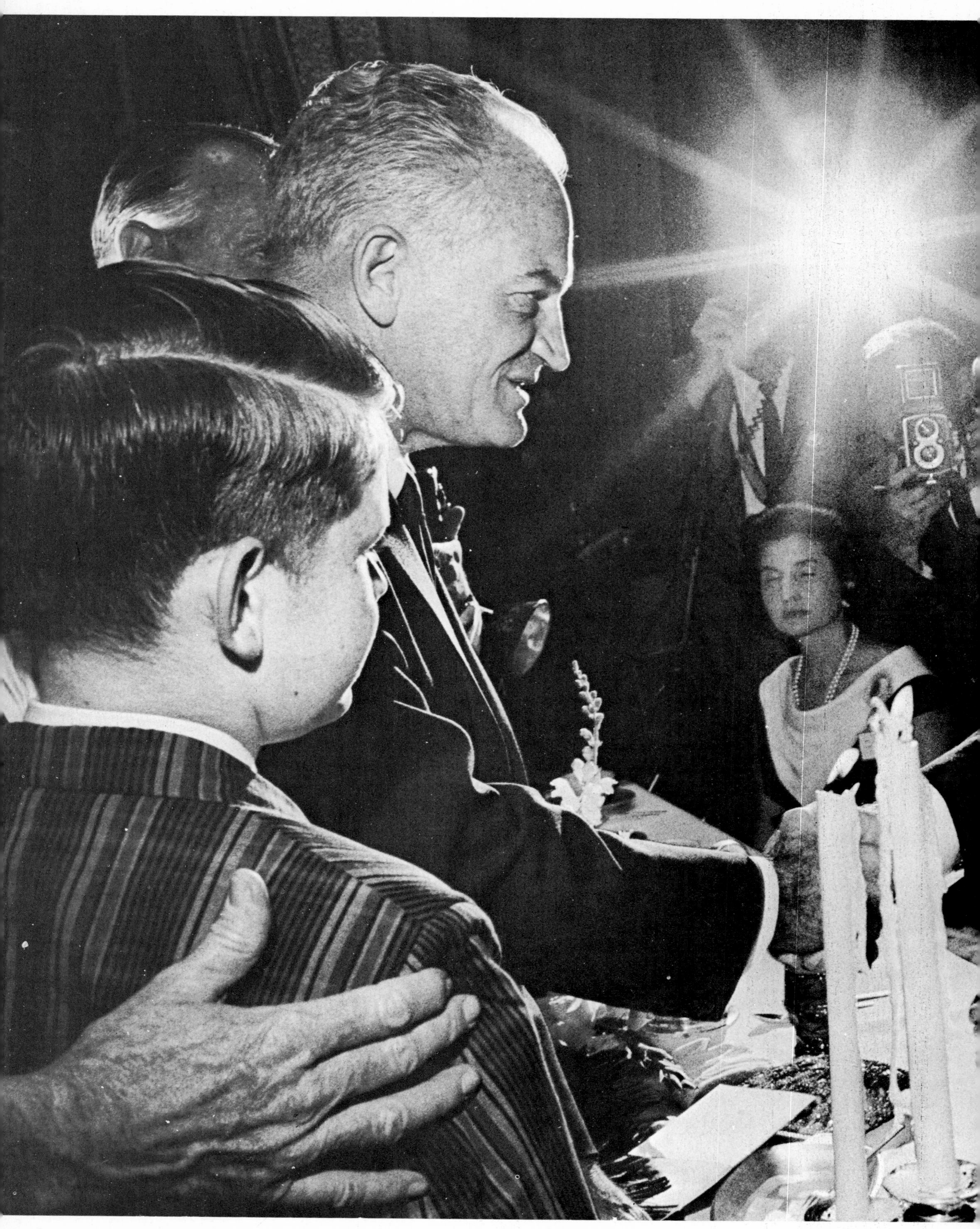

On one of his rare public forays into politics after leaving the Presidency, Ike shakes hands with Barry Goldwater at the 56th annual Governors' Conference in Cleveland in 1964, a month before Goldwater was chosen the GOP Presidential candidate. A "stop-Goldwater" drive mounted at the Conference failed, partly because Ike, considered the one man who could have prevented the nomination, refused to become part of a "cabal" to block Goldwater's candidacy.

Looking contented and happy, Ike and Mamie sit together (right) on the lawn behind their home in the evening, enjoying one of the pleasures of life on the farm. At left, the former President proudly leads an Arabian mare. The picture below shows the horse barn (rear) and the tree-shaded house; the farm is close to the Gettysburg battlefield, not far from where Confederate General George Pickett began his famous charge.

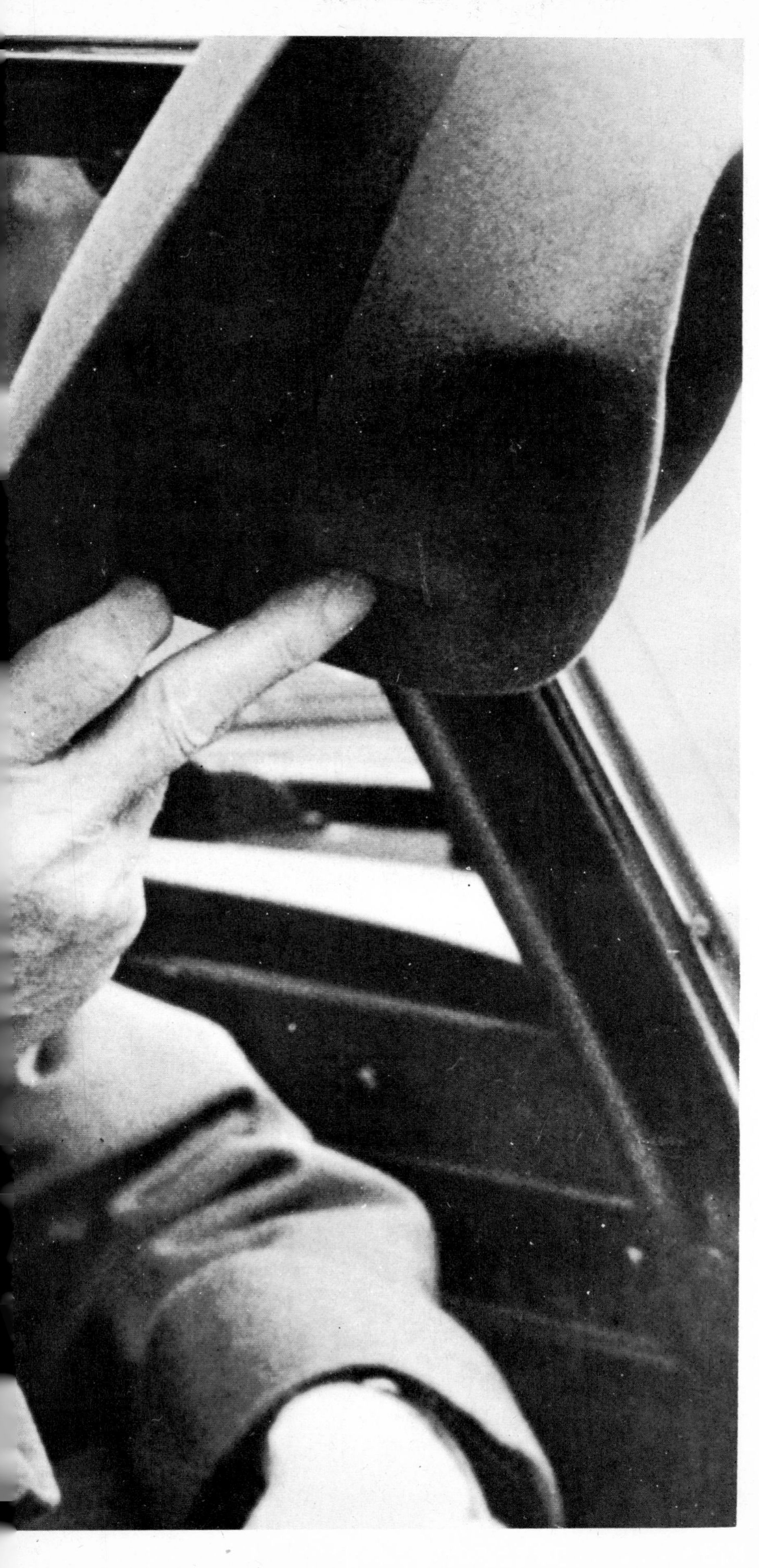

With a gallant tip of his hat and a flash of the famous smile that brought him countless friends throughout the world, Ike bids farewell to a photographer who came to see him in Gettysburg shortly before he entered the hospital in 1966 for removal of his gall bladder. Throughout his many illnesses—even in his last weeks, when he underwent emergency intestinal surgery, contracted pneumonia and finally suffered congestive heart failure—the former President fought for his life with characteristic tenacity; until his death on March 28, 1969, he remained optimistic and indomitable.

IKE—SEEN BY ONE OF HIS OFFICIAL FAMILY

10

When I think about Dwight Eisenhower, I like to recall an incident that took place aboard the Presidential yacht *Williamsburg* shortly after he was inaugurated for his first term in 1953. The *Williamsburg,* a handsome little vessel, was being used as a sort of recreational ship for GIs who had been injured during the Korean War. The customary routine was to get underway in the early afternoon and cruise to Mount Vernon and back, arriving at the dock in the Washington Navy Yard in time for a bus ride to Walter Reed Hospital and a late supper. During the trip the patients had the freedom of all parts of the ship, including the Presidential suite, as well as an abundance of soft drinks and food. For the first of these trips the President came down to the ship to welcome the soldiers and bid them a pleasant afternoon.

As Eisenhower boarded the *Williamsburg,* he stepped in among the soldiers, brushing aside his Secret Service guards with words to the effect, "Just let me be for a while. I know these men."

The soldiers crowded in around him. They were young men whose bodies had been ravaged by war in some way; some lacked an arm or a leg, some hobbled on crutches, others had heartbreaking facial disfigurements. One clean-cut chap had an attendant who never left his side; there was a huge depression in his forehead. They gathered as close to the President as they could get, and I heard him talking to them.

This was an Eisenhower that the public never saw. He talked to the soldiers of love of country, and of sacrifice. He said their country would never let them down, but no matter how much it did for them it was as nothing compared to what they had done for it. And then he said that even with all they had already given, they must yet be prepared to give even more, for they were symbols of devotion and sacrifice and they could never escape that role and its responsibilities.

His voice had a deep friendly warmth, with a somewhat different timbre than I had ever heard before. It reached out and grabbed the men around him, so that they kept crowding in closer and closer as he talked, as if an unseen magnet were pulling at them.

At the time the President visited the *Williamsburg,* I had been on his staff only a few months. Over the next four years, I saw him under the terrible pressures of his office, including the continuing Cold War with Russia, the Hungarian uprising, the Suez affair and the two major illnesses he suffered during his first term. I saw the President in many moods, jovial, thoughtful, sad—and more than once angry.

Through all of these various crises, I never ceased to have the greatest affection and respect, bordering on devotion, for Dwight Eisenhower. As a man, he was kind, generous, considerate of others and approachable—so long as you did not waste his time. As the nation's Chief Executive, he showed the greatest restraint and delicacy in dealing with the sensibilities that ran the world's affairs. This was brought home to me in comments of British officials after the Suez crisis of 1956. He was a person of tremendous integrity, selflessly dedicated to his office and determined to use the awesome power of the Presidency in an effort to strengthen the nation and further the cause of world peace.

While my primary duty was to provide liaison between the Navy and the White House, I was also placed in charge of civil defense for the White House. This assignment quickly broadened to considerations of the continuity of the government under atomic attack, and in this role I soon had an opportunity to see how the President thought and functioned.

One of my first responsibilities was to devise a plan to provide headquarters for the President—an alternate, protected White House—in case Washington came under attack. After about a year of work, I brought two architects' plans to the President. Eisenhower approved the more economical of the two layouts, but then he hesitated. Finally he said that though he knew this was far more than just a White House shelter, still, it would look like one and inevitably be so called. As President, he said, he could not build himself a shelter when other Americans did not have them. He could not, as President, expend public funds for his personal protection against the type of attack we were talking about.

His advisers pointed out that the emergency headquarters was not just to protect him, as an individual, but to insure the continuity of government, regardless of who was President. The President answered, with some heat, that of course he knew that, but people would not believe it; furthermore, he added (and suddenly it was the general speaking) he would not leave the city when it was under attack.

It took a moment for the full implication of his words to sink in. Then Dr. Arthur S. Flemming, head of the Office of Defense Mobilization, said what we were all thinking: "Mr. President, that's not your choice. It's the government we're thinking about. We might even have to *force* you to go!" The President grinned in a peculiar thin-lipped way, and suddenly I knew what he was thinking: "Just *who* did you say was going to force me?"

In the end, he agreed to have the headquarters built—but required that plans for the removal of himself and his staff to it go forward only as part of a much larger plan: to have the entire population of Washington evacuated in case of enemy attack. Until then, said he firmly, he would not go.

I had long heard that Eisenhower was personally extremely efficient and did not take kindly to having his time wasted. Soon after joining his staff I had a forceful and embarrassing demonstration of this. As his Naval Aide, part of my job was to make appointments for him when they concerned naval affairs. The first appointment I set up was memorable, to me at least. More precisely, it was a disaster.

A highly placed admiral in the Navy Department asked me to arrange for the President to meet an industrialist of importance to the Navy. I duly called Tom Stephens, the Appointment Secretary, made the necessary arrangements and received at the same time Tom's admonition to "get him out on time."

At the specified hour my man came to my office. We talked briefly and he seemed urbane and intelligent. I explained how important the President's time was; from the depths of my own anxiety I contrived a scheme for terminating the interview if necessary. Casually I mentioned that I, too, had a small matter I wished to discuss with the President. I minimized its significance and said I could find another time for it, but I added that I would be grateful for the opportunity to bring it up at this occasion, should the time permit.

I had some idea that this would make it easier for me to interrupt at the end of our allotted time, but almost from the beginning, everything went wrong. Stephens ushered us into the President's office and threw us off stride at once by fiddling with papers on Eisenhower's desk and discussing one or two matters he wanted to bring up. Finally, with a meaningful look at me and another at his wristwatch, he departed. The President motioned my man to a chair alongside his desk and I drew up a small one several feet to the rear. To my consternation, my urbane industrialist stuttered something to the effect that while he had many significant things to discuss with the President, his aide—myself—had an even more important item to bring up first.

Caught totally by surprise, I lamely tried to marshal my thoughts. It was a poor effort. Eisenhower's eyes turned quizzical as he looked at me. Finally the horrible moment ended and the President's attention returned to his visitor. But the cogent, logical-minded businessman with whom I had been talking for several minutes had suddenly lost his tongue. He stuttered some hardly intelligible words of congratulations on Eisenhower's election, stared into the distance and mumbled a few more almost incoherent phrases. At this point the President suddenly leaped to his feet, thrust out his hand, thanked the visitor warmly for coming to see him, and firmly escorted us to the door, opened it, and bowed us out. To put it bluntly, we had been kicked out.

While the President invariably treated outsiders with courtesy and restraint, he was frequently much more blunt with his staff. All of us realized the unrelenting pressure he was under; if we did not welcome being the occasional target of his wrath, at least we tried to understand that it served a therapeutic purpose and waited philosophically for the storm to blow itself out.

One time I felt the President's wrath was when I had the unpleasant duty of bringing him pictures that the Navy had just released to the newspapers. The photographs showed a still-secret airplane, and they had not been intended for publication. They had been hurriedly released because a West Coast newspaper had "sneaked" some pictures of the plane. Apparently the Navy's sudden action was meant to deprive the one newspaper of a scoop and thus discourage other journalists from attempting similar circumventions of security regulations. But the officials responsible had overlooked the additional —and far more serious—consequences of their hasty step. The Navy release gratuitously confirmed information that had been kept carefully secret, and even called the whole world's attention to it.

This type of offense—an apparently irresponsible or

stupid damage to national security—brought the Presidential reaction we had learned to watch for. Eisenhower's mouth tightened in a characteristic way. The voice was cold and aloof, but his face was red with anger, telltale touches of gray under the eyes, as if fury had drained the blood from the skin. He virtually ground his teeth together as he strode around the room berating me for the Navy's inexcusable unwisdom—to use a mild word for what he spelled out at length and in detail—in permitting photographs of intelligence value to get out. Though I could reflect that I had had nothing personally to do with the situation and that the President's anger was not directed toward me personally, since I was the Navy's representative, I was the target. I braced myself for the storm and took its fury.

All of us around the President at one time or another had occasion to experience these sudden bursts of temper. Usually they came without warning, were expressive, as were so many things, of his quickness of reaction. They subsided just as rapidly as they arose and we soon learned that for him they were a sort of release.

Nearly all of the difficult problems he was attempting to solve involved at their core the matter of human relationships, and his philosophy required that in such areas he maintain his temper at all costs. Patience was the formula he sought under all circumstances. Such patience meant, among other things, that he could never give vent to his true inner feelings outside his own official circle. What it cost him only we in the White House knew—and I think some of us sometimes almost welcomed serving as the catalyst for the release of some of the tensions caused by others.

There is always a danger that members of the staff of a much admired boss will ascribe superhuman qualities to him. It is therefore with some trepidation that one of President Eisenhower's pronounced personal characteristics—the quickness of his mind—is cited. Yet every member of Eisenhower's staff experienced this rapidity of reaction and commented upon it. That this same characteristic was less well observed by the press and the public at large obviously demands some explanation.

Long ago he learned to distrust the "flash" decision. If there was time for planning, he insisted that this vital staff work be performed before any decision of importance. Once the thorough thinking had been done, decision and action could come swiftly, and the results could be trusted. It was not that advice was unanimous. On the contrary, this was a rarity. The point was that every such decision—which only the President could make—was made with awareness of all sides of the issue.

One example was the termination of the Korean War. It is now customary to suggest that during his first Presidential campaign Eisenhower "promised," if elected, to end this unpopular war. This view is not correct; what he did was to commit himself to a searching examination of it. The novelty of the undertaking, the then-existing misconceptions of the "Communist Monolith" and Chinese war power, the complication of concerting action with the other U.N. forces and the stern refusal of South Korea's aged president to tolerate any cessation of fighting except on the basis of complete victory, made this an extraordinarily difficult task. The brunt of it fell on the National Security Council and its Planning Board. It was not something upon which he could have, or should have, reached a decision overnight. New issues continued to arise. Singhman Rhee—a brave man dedicated to his country's salvation—continued to be intractable, and a special ambassador had to be flown to Korea to deal with his incredible threat to "go it alone." The result of it all, while perhaps not the world's best peace, has endured for years.

Another example was the Suez crisis of 1956. Even greater speed of reaction was necessary, for here the balloon really seemed about to go up. The atmosphere in the White House, especially in the west wing where the Cabinet room and the President's office were located, grew tenser by the hour. The Cabinet table, under the solemn visage of the portrait of Lincoln, was in almost continual use. The Dulles brothers, the Chairman of the Joint Chiefs of Staff, the Vice President, the Chairman of the Atomic Energy Commission, the Secretary of Defense, all came and departed quietly, gravely. The White House telephone switchboard went into double overtime operation, and the phone lines overseas were almost never dead.

As this situation developed I could see that Eisenhower was pulled two ways at once. His personal and immediate reaction to the Egyptian seizure of the Suez Canal was natural sympathy with Britain and France. After all, they had built the Canal and successfully operated it for nearly a century. Well did he recognize what that Canal meant historically and economically to his old comrades in arms and to the nations and peoples he had helped to free from tyranny such a short time ago. He strongly disagreed, however, with the British and French action, and I could read his feelings in his face and eyes as the weight of the logic and arguments of his most senior staff advisers convinced him of the course the U.S. must take. The considered verdict of history will undoubtedly be that our action was the right one. War was averted, lives were saved, and the Suez Canal was restored to use of the world's traffic and the loudly voiced fears that Egypt could not run it efficiently proved incorrect.

I went back to sea early in 1957 and consequently can relate the third example, the revolt that exploded in Iraq in 1958, only from secondhand—though unimpeachable—authority. This blow-up did much more than destroy the government of Iraq; it cast a terrible doubt whether Lebanon and Jordan, and perhaps even Israel, might not also be engulfed. On the same day as the Iraqi outbreak, our State Department received an appeal from Lebanon, in accordance with formal agreement, for immediate military assistance in time of crisis. It was an emergency, and the President met it head-on. Our Sixth Fleet, normally stationed in the Mediterranean, was ordered to steam toward Lebanon, stay out of sight of land and await orders. A National Security Council meeting happened to be scheduled for that very morning. The President, presiding as he always did, permitted only one short item to be heard. Then he terminated the meeting, called certain members into his office and reconvened it.

A nearly similar situation had arisen only a year earlier. He listened to the Secretary of State's appreciation of the situation, to the report from the intelligence community, and to the Chairman of the Joint Chiefs of Staff. It was clear to all that if prompt action were not taken on Lebanon's call for help, that little nation would be in grave danger of quick collapse; so would Jordan, already under threat, her king on an assassination list. Action, if it were to be taken, had to be taken immediately; time used in debating would be time given away to those hostile to peace in the world. The best way to forestall a sudden holocaust was to act before the contagion could spread throughout the Middle East. It was imperative to move before the U.S.S.R. had time, by its own intervention, to turn the situation into a confrontation.

The meeting lasted one hour. At its close, Eisenhower ordered that U.N. Ambassador Henry Cabot Lodge be advised to state the U.S. position to the U.N. on the next day and that Congressional leaders be invited to the White House after lunch so that he could inform them in person. Then he directed the Chairman of the Joint Chiefs of Staff to take immediate action on land, sea and air. A few hours later, as dawn crept from Lebanon into the sea, the morning sun reflected from the gray hulls of ships of the Navy, standing close inshore, well in sight of land. Carrier aircraft flew overhead in military formation. A little later, landing craft boiled through the water to the beaches and the first 1,700 Marines in battle dress waded ashore. Russia, if she had had any schemes to become involved in the situation, held her hand. Lebanon and Jordan remained free, their governments undisturbed. No blood was shed; and a few months later the Marines departed, leaving Lebanon intact.

Everyone who writes about President Eisenhower will have his own special anecdote most clearly illustrating the kind of man he was, and providing, perhaps for that individual alone, the wellsprings of those factors that for him epitomize the character of the 34th President of the United States. For me this episode was the President's trip to Panama in July 1956, for the inter-American conference there. Eisenhower's decision to be a candidate for a second term had been announced and then, in June 1956, he had to undergo an ileitis operation. Next month he was off to Panama.

For a man only recently out of the hospital, the trip turned out to be more of an ordeal than he had bargained for. Watching with concern and growing pride, I saw the President repeatedly display the qualities that had served him so well throughout his long career: ability to remain patient even under trying—and unexpected—circumstances, consideration for the men who served him, a sly touch of humor, his personal humility and determination to see through to the end any job he undertook, regardless of personal discomfort.

We landed in Panama on a broiling-hot summer day and climbed into the caravan of cars prepared for us for an hour-long procession through the city. But this was nothing compared to the procession to the formal meeting the next day. Obviously our departure time and route had been well advertised. Slowly, with the President's car in the lead, the procession wound its way through the narrow streets of Panama City. Probably no one had fully anticipated what a wildly enthusiastic reception President Eisenhower would receive. Everywhere within the city our route was jammed with people completely blocking the streets from building to building on either side. The Panamanian police strove valiantly to clear a way through the friendly throng, with only partial success. Everyone in Panama, it seemed, wanted to touch the President's car, wave at him, see him personally from up close. Heedlessly they pressed toward his moving limousine.

As the cheering, enthusiastic Panama crowds forced the caravan to slow to a crawl, the doors of both sides of the following Secret Service cars popped open, and out jumped the Secret Service men who ranged themselves on either side of the President's limousine, jogging along with it. While the situation that had developed was not entirely unexpected, no one had really anticipated crowds so big. The agents, obeying their orders to stay between the crowd and the President at all times, had no choice but to run on the pavement alongside. (There were then no running boards on the Presidential car, as there are now.)

The Secret Service men, dressed in conservative business suits, complete with shirt, tie and shoulder holster, must have run several miles through the sweltering heat and humidity. At intervals, one of them would hop into a follow-up car for a few minutes to catch his breath, being relieved by the man who had just preceded him.

Then I noticed something. Every once in a while when the President's car stopped, the door would open A Secret Service man, unseen heretofore, would scramble out and another would crawl in and disappear. The President was inviting his sweating, gasping protectors, singly and in pairs, into his car where they lay on the floor, invisible to the crowd, breathing heavily, their clothes soaked through with perspiration, their athletic aroma rising in a miasma of vapor in his face. Then after a short respite, they would be out and running alongside again.

Through most of that interminable two-hour ride through the streets of Panama, while many thousands of people screamed a delighted welcome to the President of the United States, there was a Secret Service man collapsed at his feet. It was he who had given the order for them to be admitted to the car for respite, and frequently he bent over and opened the door for them himself. Except for these moments, however, as he rode with his benign, open countenance, his friendly wave, his delighted response to those welcoming him so vociferously, there was not the slightest indication that he had any awareness whatsoever of the truly remarkable effort being put on by these men whose duty was to protect the President at all costs.

But this was only one of the ordeals of the trip to Panama. A plenary council of the chiefs of state was held in an ancient Spanish-style building in the old part of town. With typical South American hospitality, each president was ceremoniously shown to his proper place at a massive table in a large hall. President Arias opened the meeting by announcing that Panama had issued a special set of commemorative stamps in honor of the historic conference, that this was their first day of issue and that a picture of each chief of state was shown on one of the stamps. A packet of stamps was at each place, and each visiting leader was asked to inscribe his name alongside the stamps bearing his likeness. Arias had also brought along a number of extra packets, and they too had to be signed. For the next hour the august heads of the American nations passed along the packets and signed their names. The packets signed, President Arias rapped for order and declared the meeting adjourned. Eisenhower took the whole thing in reasonably good spirits, though he could not resist grumbling to Secretary of State John Foster Dulles, in an aside later, that the business of the conference seemed to be for the chiefs of state to sign their names over and over again for a bunch of stamp collectors.

The situation was somewhat retrieved that night when Eisenhower gave a dinner for Arias in the American Embassy and later was able to have a couple of hours of discussion on the specific problems of Panama. Predictably, these talks involved the Canal and the annual revenue derived from it by the Republic of Panama.

During the stay in Panama the only concession the President made to his recent illness was to take a nap after lunch. One day I accompanied the President to his room. He was in a talkative mood and I lingered while he changed into his pajamas. I no longer remember what he said, but he was completely unself-conscious as he disrobed and revealed a large bandage on his abdomen where the ileitis operation had been performed. I was astonished to observe not only that the incision had not yet healed, but that it was, in fact, still draining slightly. The President seemed oblivious of the wound, neither concealing nor calling attention to it, as he changed the dressing. Off-handedly, he motioned negatively when I moved to help him with it.

I believe this little episode was representative of his attitude toward himself and the Presidency as well. During all of his illnesses he insisted on the full disclosure of his condition to the public—probably a carry-over from his military training that an officer must keep his superiors informed about his exact condition. And certainly it was another demonstration of his refusal to spare himself in fulfilling all of the obligations of his office.

The grand finale of the sojourn in Panama was the official signing of the Declaration of the Presidents, followed by the usual speeches that accompany such occasions. Everyone had been carefully briefed to take no more than six minutes.

For a while all went according to schedule. Then Fulgencio Batista, at the time dictator of Cuba, stepped forward and spoke for nearly 20 minutes. When Eisenhower's turn came he completed his remarks in five minutes. From my post standing behind the President, I soon began surreptitiously timing the speeches; almost immediately the roof caved in when a spare Spanish grandee-type talked for 47 minutes, gesturing vigorously toward the heavens above and the regions below. During this marathon speech, our Secret Service men kept running back and forth behind the platform, consulting with President Arias. Finally one of the agents came to me and whispered Arias' message that in view of President Eisenhower's recent illness no one would think it amiss if he bade the assembly goodby and departed.

I duly relayed the suggestion to Eisenhower. At that time I had been standing in a rigid posture of attention for almost two hours, and my feet were sore. Even so, I hoped he would not agree to leave. He looked up at me, his face glistening with sweat. He was visibly irritated by having to sit through a long harangue that he could not understand, made unconscionably longer by thoughtlessness. His answer was spit forth at me almost as though I had proposed surrendering to the Germans: it was unmistakably clear, and not exactly in diplomatic language. He would do no such thing as leave. That wasn't what he had come for. He would make no concessions that might in any way compromise his office or the effect of the visit.

Strangely, my feet were less sore, and it was easier to stand at rigid attention after that. For the next hour and a half the speeches went on. Unable to follow them, the President began to study the crowd. His eye picked up three women in white nuns' habits sitting in the middle of the throng. One of the nuns reached inside her bodice, pulled out a tiny American flag, waved it rapidly two or three times and then tucked it out of sight. The gesture delighted the President. He beamed and waved his thanks. The nuns whispered self-consciously to each other, and then looked around to see if there might have been someone else to whom he had waved. A few minutes later out came the little flag again, back and forth it went quickly, almost surreptitiously, and then again it disappeared. Eisenhower responded with another wave and pointed to them. The good sisters were convulsed with joy, embarrassment and giggles.

After the speeches finally ended, I asked one of the Secret Service agents to bring the nuns to meet the President. It turned out that they were all Americans who had worked in Panama for several years. It was like the President to find pleasure and wry amusement in an unexpected incident that broke the monotony of a trying ceremonial occasion, and the nuns undoubtedly had a story that they could tell their comrades for years.

I noted, however, that in speaking to them the President made no allusion to the fact that they had helped him pass the time during the preposterous and interminable period. When he commented on it later he said that of course he was grateful to them, but they would tell their friends about seeing him, and if he mentioned this they would repeat it. If the story became public it might work detriment to some of the good he was trying to accomplish by the trip.

A short time after the Panama visit my tour of duty ended, and I left the White House staff to go back to sea. No one can profess to predict how history will treat Dwight Eisenhower as President, what final judgments it will make about him, but I know what it ought to say: here was one of the truly great men of his time. I saw what he did and how he acted in office. There is no question in my own mind but that President Eisenhower felt himself in the forefront of the battle for a better world and viewed his illness as analogous to the injuries of combat. Under him the entire Executive Department functioned as a well-coordinated staff with established lines of responsibility and clear-cut channels by which the Chief Executive's decision could be obtained. Under him the nation progressed decisively, yet always in harmony with the long-established American traditions that give the country its intrinsic stability.

To me it was a great privilege to have served under Dwight Eisenhower, an exciting and rewarding experience for which I will always be grateful. I shall remember him not just as a figure who wielded tremendous power and helped shape the events of our time, but as a man of good will who, despite his high position, his great personal popularity and international celebrity, never forgot his essential humanity and that of the people with whom he lived and worked—and who worked for him.

CREDITS

The sources for the illustrations in this book are shown below. Credits for the pictures from left to right are separated by commas, from top to bottom by dashes.

Cover:
Hank Walker

Chapter 1: 9—George Downing, Topeka, Kansas. 10—Edward Clark. 11—Jeffcoat from Monkmeyer Press Photo Service. 14—Bottom; Wide World Photos. 16-17—Brown Brothers.

Chapter 2: 18—European. 2C—Harris and Ewing. 21—from *The Howitzer*, 1915. 22, 23—courtesy John Eisenhower. 28, 29—Culver Pictures, the Baltimore Sun Papers. 30—courtesy Fox B. Conner. 32, 33—Right; Jeffcoat Studio and Camera Shop.

Chapter 3: 36 through 39—United Press International. 41—Left; courtesy John Eisenhower. 42, 43—Right; United Press International.

Chapter 4: 44—Margaret Bourke-White. 46, 47—Ralph Morse. 48, 49—Wide World Photos, United Press International—official U.S. Navy photograph. 50, 51—Wide World Photos. 52, 53—Imperial War Museum, London. 54, 55—U.S. Army photograph, Eliot Elisofon—Wide World Photos. 56—U.S. Army photograph. 58, 59—Signal Corps photo, Eliot Elisofon. 60, 61—Imperial War Museum, London.

Chapter 5: 62, 63—Gordon Coster. 64, 65—United Press International, Wide World Photos—Frank Scherschel. 66, 67—Bottom left; Neal Slavin, U.S. Army photograph except center; Signal Corps photo. 68, 69—Robert Capa—U.S. Coast Guard. 70—United Press International—Frank Scherschel. 71—U.S. Army photograph, Frank Scherschel—Signal Corps photo, Wide World Photos—British Information Services. 73—Bob Landry. 74—Wide World Photos. 75—U.S. Army photograph. 76, 77—Left; Signal Corps photos (2)—U.S. Army photograph, Ralph Morse. 79—Edward Clark.

Chapter 6: 80—© Arnold Newman. 82, 83—United Press International, Irving Hamberger, United Press International—Columbia University photo by Warman. 85—David Douglas Duncan. 86—United Press International. 87—Wide World Photos. 88—I. Sy Seidman and Culver Pictures, cartoon by Jay N. Darling reproduced with permission of W.C.C. Publishing Company, Inc. 89—United Press International. 90—Wide World Photos—Alfred Eisenstaedt. 91—Alfred Eisenstaedt. 92, 93—Wide World Photos except top left; Joe Scherschel.

Chapter 7: 94—Mark Kauffman. 97—Leonard McCombe, United Press International. 98, 99—Hank Walker. 101—© 1955 by The New York Times Company; reprinted by permission, Carl Iwasaki. 102—United Press International. 103—Abbie Rowe courtesy National Park Service. 104, 105—Larry Burrows—Erich Lessing from Magnum, United Press International. 106—Wide World Photos. 107—United Press International.

Chapter 8: 108, 109—Hank Walker. 112,113—John Bryson—George Silk, John Bryson. 114, 115—Hank Walker except top right; Hanson Carroll. 116—U.S. Army photograph. 118, 119—James Burke—Paul Schutzer. 120, 121—Left; Alfred Eisenstaedt, Howard Sochurek—Carl Mydans. 122, 123—Paul Schutzer, Edward Clark—Frank Scherschel. 124, 125—Edward Clark.

Chapter 9: 126—Wide World Photos. 128, 129—United Press International. 130—Wide World Photos. 131—Brian Seed—Alan Clifton. 132, 133—Bill Eppridge. 134, 135—Edward Clark. 136, 137—Wide World Photos.

PRODUCTION STAFF FOR TIME INCORPORATED

John L. Hallenbeck (Vice President and Director of Production), Robert E. Foy and Caroline Ferri

Text photocomposed under the direction of Albert J. Dunn and Arthur J. Dunn